ZERO COST ECONOMICS

AN INTRODUCTION TO THE ECONOMICS OF AN ECONOMY

Dr. Farid A. Khavari

Unconventional Economist
"Creator of Zero Cost Economics"

*Karl Marx, John Maynard Keynes, and Milton Friedman utterly **failed** in their economic theories, leaving a legacy of flawed ideas and missed opportunities!*

ISBN: 978-1-963919-68-4

An Important Note

During the first presidential debate on June 25, 2024, CNN anchor Jake Tapper asked both candidates, former President Donald J. Trump and President Joe Biden, repeatedly:

"What would you do to improve American people's life?"

Here is an introduction to a new economic model, Zero Cost Economics (Public Capitalism), to improve the life of all American people because both conventional economic models, liberal and conservative, have failed miserably. The future outcomes of their implementation will be increasingly worse, leading to the collapse of the world economies altogether.

An Open Letter To President Donald J. Trump

Dear President Trump:

First and foremost, I am relieved and glad to know that you are safe and healthy after the two vicious assassination attempts on you. All indications are that you will win the presidential election in November 2024. Please allow me to congratulate you in advance. But, more importantly, I would like the opportunity to help make your presidency a great success with an effective, coherent, and comprehensive economic plan.

Of course, you have a huge burden to carry, not only to resolve the woes of our nation but also to make our once great nation great again.

Unfortunately, you have only four short years to accomplish it, and experience has proven that conventional economic models, whether liberal or conservative, do not work.

All conventional economic models are inflationary and debt-inducing, and they work for only a few groups, not for all people. Without making all Americans great, America cannot become great.

Even if you send all the illegal immigrants back to their origins and reduce inflation, it is simply impossible for all financially suffering Americans to achieve a decent living standard with economic and financial security by using policies based on conventional economics.

The biggest challenge to your presidency would be the declining living standards of Americans and the rise of associated social costs. This would be much worse than the rising national debt because it would immediately affect all American families.

At the same time, we face many other challenges, including de-dollarization efforts of the BRICS-Nations, housing, energy, agriculture, healthcare, raw materials, military threats, natural disasters, retirement, income and wealth, Middle East and world crises, and most importantly, the recurring and rising social costs associated with these and other factors of the economy.

Zero Cost Economics can provide effective solutions for many of the economic challenges with zero net costs by converting rising recurring social costs of all kinds into rising general prosperity and economic and financial security for all our people.

I have written a five-part book to contribute to the success of your administration in devising a prudent, coherent, and comprehensive plan covering economics, monetary policy, oil and energy, the Middle East, counter-de-dollarization, foreign policy, agriculture, environmental, trade, natural disaster, and other vital issues.

This brief paper covers the relevant concepts and subjects of my current work. My biography, with an overview of my past works and qualifications, is attached.

I am not applying for a position in your administration; I just want to make your presidency successful.

Sincerely,

Farid A. Khavari, PhD.

Unconventional Economist

Creator of Zero Cost Economics

A Plea to American Voters

The Biden-Harris Administration has led America into a very dangerous situation, with inflation, illegal immigration, high energy and food prices, and lack of affordable housing — in short, Bidenomics. The worst is yet to come if Kamala Harris is elected as the next U.S. president.

No Americans who care about themselves, their families, and our country should want Kamala Harris as the next U.S. president, which could be the end of America as we know it. You may already feel that you are living in a strange country.

Before the Biden-Harris Administration and the Democratic Party can give mass amnesty to illegal immigrants and give them resources that deprive needy Americans, we have only one hope to get America back on track: President Donald Trump.

President Trump may not be able to make America perfect, but he'll be far better than Kamala Harris or any other Democrats. And what a nightmare it will be if Kamala Harris is elected, and we are stuck with her grating laugh and no useful substance of any kind for the next four years.

I ask all Americans, Democrats, Independents, Republicans, of all races and backgrounds, in the interests of themselves, their families and friends, and the continued existence of

America as we know it, to vote without hesitation for President Donald J. Trump.

But remember, electing President Trump with a landslide victory is not enough to guarantee his success to make America and Americans great again. We need a Republican majority in both Houses of Congress as well.

This paper is a brief overview of a forthcoming series of four books. It is intended as a guideline to a great future for all Americans and a new economic model for the world to emulate.

We must create a peaceful and prosperous world, and why not start with the United States of America? America is a beautiful country with the most tolerant people in the world. Let's all come together and save it.

Thank you.

Farid A. Khavari, PhD.

Unconventional Economist

Creator of Zero Cost Economics

A Necessary Explanation To All Democrats

The sole reason for not offering this book to Vice President Kamala Harris and her running mate, Governor Tim Walz, is simply because of my conviction based on the past three and half years of my close observation of the Biden-Harris Administration's frustrating records that clearly demonstrated neither one of them have the interests of American people in mind other than the drive of the party leaders to consolidate power and realize their agenda, which would take this great nation to an uncertain future.

Realizing this reality, I concluded it would be a waste of time and energy to do so, but I feel that I owe an explanation to all Democrats, whether they welcome it or not.

Worse, neither Vice President Kamala Harris nor Governor Tim Walz would have the intellectual capacity to understand the necessity to implement the concept and recommendations presented in this book; deficit-spending and conventional economics are both failed concepts because they are both inflationary and debt-inducing. Unfortunately, the agenda they have based on the past three and half years is not in the interest of the American people, regardless of whether they are Democrats, Republicans, or Independents! But one thing is for sure: both the party leadership and Kamal Harris want all the votes they can get from all groups of people so that Kamala Harris can become the next president of the United States and realize their agenda to consolidate their power for good.

One fact that nobody can dispute is if someone does not have any clue or interest in a subject, no matter how much effort one makes in explaining it to an ignorant person, it will be rejected or ignored. This was another reason for my reaction.

However, nobody will be deprived of acquiring this book, including Vice President Kamala Harris, Governor Tim Walz, and all other Democrats, in the same way it is available to all other people anywhere in the world.

It would be no exaggeration, and it is not farfetched at all to say that by implementing Zero Cost Economics, no ruler of this world would need to employ all kinds of wrong moves to consolidate power and maintain their grip on power.

Thank you!

Farid A. Khavari, PhD.

Unconventional Economist

Creator of Zero Cost Economics

The most difficult challenge in the world
is to melt a frozen mind

Dedication

This book is dedicated to Elle Alessandra, my four-and-a-half-year-old granddaughter, my only granddaughter, and to the millions, actually billions, of future infants, children, and the future young generation. They could have a much better life than we ever did if only the leaders of this world would finally wake up and realize that instead of war, killing, looting, plundering, poverty, hunger, homelessness, and ultimately self-destruction, they could implement the concepts envisioned and described in this and my other four books to create a peaceful and prosperous world for all.

We must reset the clock to peaceful and constructive work before it is too late—for the sake of Elle Alessandra and future generations.

ACKNOWLEDGEMENT

I would like to express my deepest gratitude to Sarah Young, the Project Manager, her excellent team, and Rosevelt Publishers for their dedication in transforming this manuscript into the beautiful book you are about to read.

Contents

About the Author

Dr. Farid A. Khavari, an "unconventional" economist, is the author of ten groundbreaking books and numerous articles published in the United States, Germany, the Netherlands, Switzerland, England, former Yugoslavia, and Iran (during the Shah's era).

Dr. Khavari earned his PhD in economics and political science from the University of Bremen in Germany, a Marxist institution, and his master's in economics and social sciences from the University of Hamburg, a conservative university. In his studies, he discovered that the foundations of both schools of thought are flawed and destined to fail, regardless of how they are applied—a point he elaborates on in this book.

He is ranked among the top 21st-century American economists (ranked #7). His full biography can be found starting on page 91 of this book.

ZERO COST ECONOMICS

Prosperity With Economic Security For Everyone Does Not Cost, It Pays.

We can have single-income households who can buy homes and raise families. We can have homes that one income can buy with 20-year financing. We can do this without inflation.

We can build and sustain a high standard of living for everyone without inflation. You can pay off your home while you are still young and save enough for a secure, comfortable retirement.

If a home is expensive, insurance and taxes are higher. What matters is not the price for the home but the home for the price.

All of America's biggest challenges come down to economic problems, but today's economic models are primitive, wasteful, obsolete, and inevitably lead to inflation and debt.

However, solving these problems is the biggest economic opportunity in history. Now, there is an economic system to transform those problems into lasting prosperity for everyone, even billionaires and corporations, starting with every American household.

Zero Cost Economics creates wealth and economic security for everyone. Zero Cost Economics focuses on freezing, reducing, and eliminating recurring costs of all kinds. The long-term savings create recurring additional wealth each year for households, governments, and the economy.

Zero Cost Economics is not complicated. It's easy for anyone to understand because it's just common sense.

In this brief paper, we'll look at three of our most important economic problems and zero-cost economic solutions that don't cost; they pay.

Farid A. Khavari, PhD.

Unconventional Economist

Creator of Zero Cost Economic

Preface

Conventional economics models, whether Liberal or Conservative, have failed miserably due to their inflationary and debt-inducing nature. No matter how many more times they are tried, the results will be the same. Unfortunately, inflation and debt will be worse and worse until the economies of the entire world collapse.

We must understand that no one regardless of the level of conventional economics education one has, can be qualified and competent to run even the simplest and most primitive economy. No political party is remotely equipped to do the job.

There are a series of other factors that must be learned and implemented in the correct way to make an economy work and become prosperous. Having great businesses alone does not make an economy great and prosperous. An economy is not an aggregation of businesses. An economy is PEOPLE.

Once the factors are known, the issue is how to implement them. The big challenges that we face are avoiding the roads leading away from our destination, identifying the right roads to the desired destination, and choosing the vehicles to take us there safely.

To accomplish that task, I have decided to present them in the next five books as follows:

Zero Cost Economics – An Introduction to the Economics of an Economy is the first of five books. It explains what is wrong with conventional economics—both Liberal and Conservative—and why we should implement the model of Zero Cost Economics.

Liberal Dystopia – What's Economically and Politically Wrong with The Democratic Party is book two of five. This book gives an overview of everything that is wrong with all political parties in general, with a thorough insight into the Democratic Party in particular. This book reflects the author's firsthand experience and knowledge of the issues involved.

Toward Zero Cost Economies: An Action Plan - The Road to World Peace and Prosperity Starts in The Post-Mullah Iran is book three. It reveals why the road to world peace and prosperity must start in Iran. The importance of this book can be seen in the fact that it shows how to bring stability and prosperity to all the world's economies, without a steamroller approach by powerful leaders, which never resolves anything.

If conventional politics fail to impose their will and demands on weaker people and nations, it ends up either in financial and terroristic, ruinous, and destructive activities, or in brutal and internecine wars, none of which can solve any problems.

We cannot tolerate nations ruled by thugs, killers, looters, terrorists, or incompetent and unqualified people. The process of Zero Cost Economics must begin in the United States, and the president who can accomplish it is Donald J. Trump. Unfortunately, the Democratic Party, starting with Jimmy

Carter, continued by Barak Obama and Joe Biden, have proven to be unqualified and incompetent for such a job. There are firsthand and publicly unknown facts that will be revealed in this book. Can anybody in their right mind expect anything better from Kamala Harris?

Zero Cost Economics – Making Economies Non-Inflationary, Debt-Free & Prosperous is book four. It describes the shortcomings and failures of all brands of conventional economic concepts. This clarifies the need for an effective and useful alternative: the unique concepts of Zero Cost Economics, an unconventional form of economics, which could be called "Public Capitalism," "General Capitalism," or "Carefreeism."

In fact, unlike all conventional economic books that present the "businesses" of an economy, this is the first book that demonstrates the true "economics" of an economy.

Zerocracy – Experts in Service of Building Peaceful and Prosperous Economies (book five) shows why the conventional political systems are totally useless, ineffective, and destructive, leading to rising and escalating social costs of all kinds by accelerating worldwide poverty.

It is not farfetched to say that the potential resolution of "conventional politics" is war, which only brings more destruction and, consequently, more impoverishment for the masses of people.

We must have only experts in different fields with specific plans to run the economy, not unqualified and incompetent politicians. We must create an alternative to the existing political system, which we proudly call Democracy, which is no more than the rule of majority on minority by unqualified and incompetent politicians with no plans to serve the people, only enriching themselves.

In contrast to Democracy, the alternative is qualified and competent experts with plans to serve people, which is dubbed Zerocracy. The experts are named Zerocrats.

Future peaceful and prosperous economies can only be built by patriotic Zerocrats in Zerocratic (Public Capitalistic) economies, not by socialistic and capitalistic (Elite Capitalistic) economies in democratic, authoritarian, theocratic, or any other form of existing political systems.

Since the United States will be under Republican Party control for the next four years, I would like to help with these five books, not only to save America but also to make it the greatest equitable, peaceful, and prosperous economy ever created — a political and economic paradigm for the world to emulate.

This book briefly introduces the concepts and solutions in these four books.

Farid A. Khavari, PhD.,

Unconventional Economist

Miami, FL

September 2024

Introduction

Conventional economic textbooks teach that an economy is an aggregation of businesses, whereas businesses are the most corrupt, self-destructive, and anti-economic factors. Businesses should, like all other factors of an economy, serve all the people, not the other way around.

When businesses maximize profits, much of the wealth created in the economy is concentrated in the hands of a small group of people, the rich and super-rich. As a result, a growing majority of people suffer poverty and destitution, becoming poorer. Therefore, the precise and correct definition of an economy is people, all people, not businesses.

Economic factors include energy, raw materials, agriculture, technology, environment, businesses, trade, foreign policy, transportation, government, financing, currency, healthcare, housing, education, legislation, politics, financing, interest, military, religion, and social issues, natural disasters, rich and superrich, poverty, and most importantly, the "normal recurring costs" and "recurring social costs" of all kinds which are caused by wrongly combining those economic factors.

In other words, economic factors that make an economy prosperous or impoverished depend on how these factors are combined with each other and implemented. However, the goal of any economy must be to implement prudent and effective economic-monetary measures that realize an environmentally safe, sustainable, and lasting standard of living with economic-financial security for all people. In fact, this would guarantee prosperous businesses.

"Prosperous people are the best guarantee for businesses to prosper."

Every economy continuously undergoes countless activities. Some of these activities are useful and constructive, while many are bad and destructive, as we witness every day. When these activities result from dogmas or lack of knowledge, qualifications, and competence of the people in charge, either in public or private sectors, the outcome cannot be any better. Without proper and effective knowledge, plans, and guidance, all the best intentions and efforts will lead to failure.

Unfortunately, conventional economics, liberal and conservative, are inflationary and debt-inducing, leading to rising general poverty and the eventual collapse of the businesses and the economy itself. They are both failed concepts, and no matter how many times they are tried, the outcomes are similar, with only one difference—the recurring social cost of all kinds keeps escalating and accelerating.

The effects of these two economic concepts become more painful when regular people must live on fixed incomes, with inflation constantly diminishing their purchasing power. Eventually, their living costs outstrip their income, and they spend all their savings on them. Their standard of living declines until more and more people end up on the streets or under bridges. The tragedy doesn't end here; they become rising sources of social costs of all kinds, which only keep accelerating, creating more costly challenges that become more detrimental to the economy.

The goal of an economy must be to create environmentally safe, sustainable, and lasting prosperity and economic security for all people. In such an economy, there would be no need for businesses to strive to maximize their profits; prosperous people are the best guarantee for prosperous businesses.

Maximizing profits is not only an absurd and short-sighted goal to pursue; it's also the primary source of corruption, economic woes, and environmental disasters, as we will see in this overview.

Shortcomings of Conventional Economics

Since an economy is traditionally — and wrongly — considered to be an aggregation of businesses, typical approaches used in running businesses are applied in trying to run an economy.

Former Republican Governor, current U.S. Senator, and 2012 U.S. presidential candidate Mitt Romney bragged that if elected, he would run the U.S. economy like a business. Romney was in the "Private Equity" business. He and his cronies would grab an existing business, sell off the valuable assets, fire a bunch of people, and bury the company in debt to pay the Private Equity saviors, that is, Romney and his gang, and reward the officers for letting this rape happen. Of course, in most cases, the company simply does not last for too long after the cash-out, with massive debt resolved by bankruptcy.

Romney and all private equity pirates enjoy a special tax deal created just for them by a grateful Congress so that Romney pays a lower tax rate than his personal assistant does.

If Romney tried to run the U.S. economy like his business, he would need to export the fired employees, plus retirees, disabled and sick people, prisoners, students, military, lawyers, doctors, the unemployed, veterans, service sector and government employees, politicians, cops, firefighters, homeless people, and everyone else not needed to feed the greed of Romney and his gang.

Since this is impractical, our economy must deal with all of them using failed conventional economic policies, which were created by guys like Romney in the first place.

When we add in inept policies like unrestricted open-gate welcome of unvetted immigrants, as seen during Joe Biden's presidency, it only exacerbates and drives the rise of social costs of all kinds.

For whatever reasons we choose to adhere to such inept and stupid policies, to have a successful economy, we must find ways to freeze, reduce, and eliminate social costs of all kinds that are associated with our standard of living.

The flaws of conventional economics stem from trying to apply business approaches to running the economy. At best, this allows for the measurement of a few aspects of the economy, such as "Gross Domestic Product." In fact, this approach creates a series of perverse incentives guaranteed to lead to the concentration of wealth in the hands of very few and growing debt and poverty for everyone else.

It is not farfetched to say that no economist is really an economist; they are all, at best, business administrators. If an economy is, first and foremost, people rather than just businesses, then economies must be governed by completely different mindsets, rules, and approaches than are used today. So far, this fact has eluded the great economic thinkers.

Despite the above-mentioned shortcomings, the biggest failure of conventional economists has been to come up with a coherent and comprehensive approach, concept, analysis, and plan; their works have been all piecemeal approaches, concepts, and analysis! Therefore, because of this reality, no economist can remotely have a complete understanding of the economy, which will enable him or her to devise a coherent and comprehensive economic plan to run an economy efficiently and successfully. That's why all these setbacks and failures characterize all conventional economists' failures.

In other words, an economy can be considered as a human body, consisting of all the organs: brain, heart, liver, hands and feet, other internal organs, and the rest of them. Like we have specialized doctors for each organ of the human body, such as brain surgeons, cardiologists, orthopedic doctors, proctologists, gastrologists, etc., economists have also specialized in different areas of the economy, labor economics, environment, finance, energy, etc., however, like general practicians they have learned Macro-economics and Micro-economics, which as an economist must have a general knowledge of anatomy of an economy, mostly focused on businesses, not the economy and people. That makes it clear that no conventional economist has a complete knowledge and understanding of all factors involved in an economy enabling him to make an economy run, to begin with—let alone to make it run friction-free, continuously, and successfully by creating a sustainable, safe, and lasting general prosperity in a carefree economy for all people.

Another major failing of conventional economics is the lack of understanding of the harmful role of regular recurring costs, social costs of all kinds, and the compounding effects of interest, energy, and healthcare costs during the different stages of production. However, the worst of all flaws of conventional economics is the failure to understand an economy must be built; it cannot be purchased due to its underlying permanent dynamic processes and changes.

Here are only seven principles out of many that highlight the flaws and shortcomings of conventional economics.

Gross Domestic Product (GDP)

Using metrics such as GDP (Gross Domestic Product) to measure the performance of an economy is misleading. By adding up all the dollar values of goods and services produced in a year, we get an impressive number that can be compared to that of previous years (after adjusting for inflation). However, GDP does not tell us how average people are doing or even how the economy is doing. And please note that interest charges, commissions for sales of stocks, overdraft fees, and other economically useless transactions are included in GDP calculations.

Current metrics do not differentiate between wealth-producing activities (such as manufacturing and construction) and wealth-reducing activities (such as most financial activities). Fifty years ago, 40% of the U.S. economy was based on manufacturing and 10% on finance. Today, it is 10% manufacturing and 40% financial activities.

Failure to recognize all the factors involved in an economy, many of which were mentioned above, and failure to recognize their complex interactions and interdependencies. There's more to an economy than businesses, and there is more to an economy than unemployment, inflation, and interest rates.

Failure to recognize the detrimental effects of recurring costs and social costs of all kinds eventually contributes to inflation and debt, dragging down people's standards of living, especially for older Americans on fixed incomes.

Phillips Curve

Conventional economists focus on the notorious Phillips Curve, which purports to define a "natural" correlation between unemployment and inflation. This doctrine is more of an idea because there are numerous versions of the Phillips Curve "correcting" previous versions. Central banks, including the Fed, follow this dogma to "control inflation" by raising interest rates until unemployment rises enough to curb demand so much that prices come down. Raising interest rates to fight inflation is the same as fighting fire with gasoline. Interest itself is inflationary.

There are plenty of ways to fight inflation without raising interest rates, just as there are plenty of ways to treat a sick person that do not involve leeches or bleeding them into a basin. And there are plenty of intelligent ways to avoid inflation in the first place, even if there is 100% full employment, once you look past obsolete traditional folk remedies like raising interest rates and firing people to fix inflation.

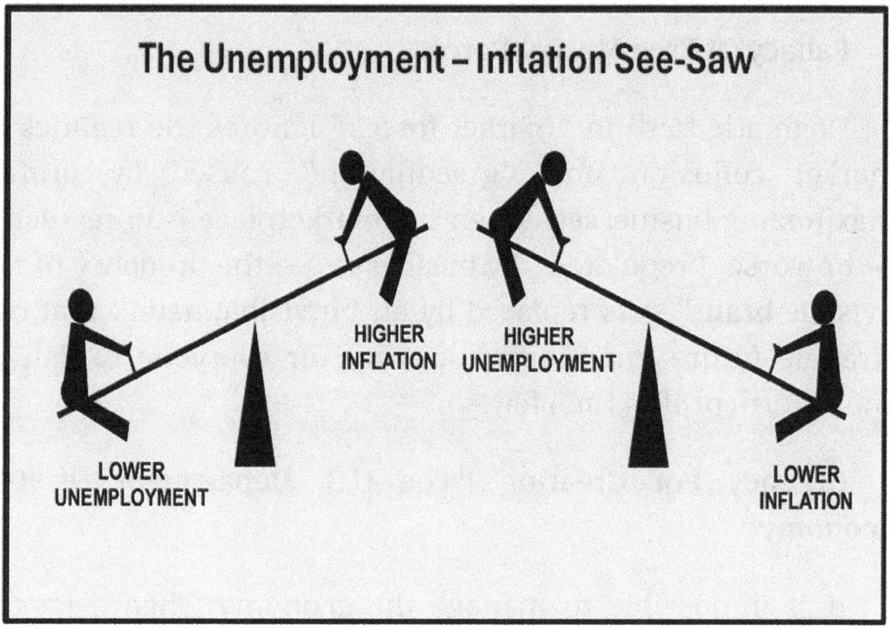

Inflation steals from everyone. The Fed's target of 2% inflation is intentionally sanctioned theft, destroys the value of savings, and entices people to make foolish and risky investments.

Zero-Inflation

The proper — and achievable — policy is to target zero inflation and a small amount of negative inflation. The price of a chicken, twenty years from now, should be the same as it is today, or a bit less. Otherwise, prudent saving for the future is useless. Even if inflation is "only" 2% for the next 20 years, in 2044, it will take $149 to buy what $100 buys today.

Fallacy Of Free Market Forces

Dogmatic faith in "market forces" ignores the realities of market collusion and "greedflation" caused by profit-maximizing businesses. When the marketplace is unregulated — or worse, "regulated" by businesses — the prudency of the "visible brain" gets replaced by an "invisible hand" that can strangle future growth and security for everyone to deliver short-term profits for a few.

Urgency For Creating "The U.S. Department Of The Economy"

It is impossible to manage the economy when even the limited levers of control are in too many unrelated hands. The Federal Reserve controls the money supply and sets interest rates. The Department of the Treasury collects taxes and pays the government's bills. The Securities and Exchange Commission is another independent institution that controls some financial markets. Congress determines tax policy and tax rates as well as various categories of business and environmental regulations in a manner that is both inefficient and openly corrupt.

Combining the functions and powers of these entities into a Department of the Economy would allow much more precise control over the economy for the benefit of the nation, all our people, and, in turn, the world economy. For example, when all the oil companies raise their prices more than their costs rise, this creates inflation. Raising interest rates and killing jobs to fight inflation just creates more inflation. Applying a windfall profits tax immediately simply ends the problem.

The Delusion Of The "Trickle-Down Economics"

The absolute stupidest idea accepted as conventional economics since 1980 is "trickle-down economics." This concept says that if you reduce taxes on the wealthy and corporations, they will invest all that extra money to "create jobs." After trillions of dollars in tax cuts over the past 44 years, there is no evidence that any of that money ever created any jobs. The actual result is trillions of dollars in additional debt plus extra donations to politicians.

The fact is that what creates jobs is demand. There will always be as many jobs as it takes to meet demand and no more. Businesses will be happy to take whatever incentives you give them, but they will not hire people if they don't need them to meet demand. These days, they may hire people in China or Vietnam rather than America.

Vicious Cycle Of Destruction

Bad things compound to make things worse in a spiral of doom. Here is an example we see every day: high interest rates raise the cost of housing. Higher home prices raise the price of insurance and property taxes. All these costs us more and more disposable income, which leaves less and less for other spending. This, in turn, reduces revenue for all businesses, which causes more unemployment, which lowers overall wages in the economy, which means fewer people can afford to buy — or even rent — homes.

What's Wrong with Business Models?

The root problem of business models is that striving to maximize profits works directly against the interests of people and the economy and, ultimately, against the interests of the business itself.

An economy includes many businesses. A business is about people, including employees and customers. Employees of one business are customers of many other businesses, and so on.

A business must serve the needs of its customers with products or services that satisfy the customers for acceptable and fair prices. A business needs to earn a reasonable profit after paying fair wages and other costs. This allows the business to continue and to grow.

The strongest economy is one where all workers have enough income to buy the goods and services they need, as well as to save for the future. In a strong economy, a variety of businesses offer goods and services, and competition assures satisfactory quality and fair prices.

If a business charges too much, competitors will undersell them. If a business does not charge enough, it won't survive. The "invisible hand" of the market will tend to optimize prices and wages, or so the theory goes. But what we need is more than the "invisible hand." We must have the "visible brain" to protect us from all the abusive and exploitative "invisible hands."

During the Great Depression in the 1930s, Henry Ford raised wages to unprecedented levels, reasoning that the survival and growth of his business depended on customers with enough money to buy his automobiles. This was radical thinking and laid the cornerstone of the Middle Class.

From the end of World War II until 1970, wages and wealth doubled for all Americans. This unprecedented prosperity resulted from the symbiotic relationship between businesses, labor, and customers. Corporations invested in communities and supported education. Families with one job bought homes, sent their kids to college, and worked until a comfortable retirement with a nice pension added to their Social Security.

Every good job creates and supports more jobs, as every paycheck circulates through the economy, a virtuous cycle.

When MAGA fans want to "make America Great Again," this is the time of greatness they dream of.

Things were going great until September 13, 1970, when the New York Times published an article by an economist from the University of Chicago named Milton Friedman. The title was "The Social Responsibility of Business is to Increase Its Profits." This concept became known as the "shareholder value" principle.

Look at the results of chasing profits and "shareholder value" in just three segments of the economy: manufacturing, housing, and health care.

Manufacturing

In 1970, 40% of the U.S. economy was based on manufacturing, and the financial sector accounted for barely 10%. Today, the financial sector accounts for 40% of the economy, and manufacturing accounts for barely 10%.

In 1970, corporations made money by manufacturing products. Corporations were run by people who knew how to make cars, appliances, machines, and so on, as well as how to build businesses that would grow and endure.

Starting in 1971, success would not be measured over the years in terms of innovative products, long-term strategy, a strong workforce, or sound, steady growth. Now, success is measured quarterly, monthly, daily, and hourly — in the price of the company's shares.

This created perverse incentives for management, and increasingly, decisions were dictated by Wall Street wizards. Corporate executives willingly obeyed Wall Street because executive pay is based on performance, meaning stock prices and the executives have stock and stock options.

There are many ways to improve short-term profits, and none of them are good for the long-term future of businesses or the economy. These include:

Delay or eliminate innovation! Developing new products and tooling up for production costs a lot! Just keep that cash, add it to the bottom line, and watch those profits and share prices soar! It's easy.

In the early 1970s, U.S. automakers built enormous cars that tended to rust and needed replacement every few years. Trying to squeeze more profits from existing products rather than innovating is how the Big 3 gave half the market to Japanese and European makers, especially when the price of gas doubled overnight in 1973.

Fire all those expensive American workers! Bust those unions! People in Mexico and China are glad to work for a fraction of what those greedy American workers demand. No need to pay pensions or health insurance for those foreigners. And those countries don't care what you dump into the river or how many low-cost workers get sick or injured. They have plenty of willing workers standing in line!

Labor is a big part of the cost of any product. Now, you can turn 90% of your labor costs directly into profits to jack up your share price and really boost your CEO's pay!

Share prices jump the minute you even announce you will be cutting payrolls, and again, each time production starts in some third-world paradise.

Eliminate overhead expenses! Let China or Mexico build and maintain the factories. Who needs the headaches, the maintenance staff, and the noise? Transfer those former costs directly to the bottom line. Send share prices and CEO pay to the moon!

Yes, we also transfer our valuable technology to those foreign countries for free. But look at all the extra shareholder value we get!

If all those cost reductions aren't enough, you can increase profits as much as you want by simply raising prices. Just blame it on inflation!

Of course, as we export more well-paying jobs, fewer paychecks circulate in America, so more and more Americans lose their jobs in all sectors of the economy. Every lost job eventually leads to another lost job, and so on: the opposite of the virtuous cycle.

All of that extra "shareholder value" may be great for Wall Street and corporate CEOs, but however much they gain, unemployment rises, social costs explode, and household and government debt skyrocket. The cost to the people and the economy is far greater than the amount of extra short-term profits for a few.

Housing

Housing is the largest cost most people pay, whether as rent or a combination of mortgage, insurance, property taxes, and maintenance.

In any case, interest affects the cost of every housing unit. For example, the difference between 4% interest and 7% makes the monthly payment — and the total cost of the house — 39% higher on a typical 30-year mortgage. Interest is the main driver of inflation in housing prices and perfect proof that interest itself is inflationary.

You might think that with over 15 million vacant housing units in the U.S. (over 10% of all units), "market forces" would push prices and rents lower. But you would think wrong. In fact, nearly half of those units are held off the market as they just gain in value.

For rental units, the average price in 1999 was about $435 ($822 in 2024 dollars) compared with $1,469 today, which is 79% higher even after counting inflation.

The average sale price in 1999 was about $95,000 ($179,550 in 2024 dollars). The average price in Q1 of 2024 was $334,800, 86% higher even after counting inflation.

Hedge funds and other greedy companies outbid individual buyers for millions of homes and now rent them out at high prices, driving up the price of houses and the cost of living. This inflation eats away at people's spending power that would support millions of other businesses and jobs, and few rich people can get even richer. In some markets, these greedy vultures snap up 30% or more of single-family homes on the market, and the share is higher every year.

Again, the total gain from the rich guys is far less than the damage done to everyone else and to our economy. Congress tried to pass a law to end this, but so far, less than $1 million in lobbying expenses has blocked it.

A potential solution could be that the new Department of the Economy could simply pass a regulation against corporate ownership of homes and slash housing costs in general by controlling rents and making low-interest mortgages available under controlled conditions.

Healthcare

Healthcare systems are another social cost-inducing, corrupt operation. Their objective is not to keep people healthy effectively but to keep them permanently sick, requiring permanent maintenance. Unfortunately, healthcare costs are the worst type of social costs because the costs keep rising with the gradual deterioration of public health. Even worse, economists think healthcare costs boost the GDP, whereas they are the worst social costs, which must be deducted from the GDP. The problem with this mindset is that our GDP has increased because of rising healthcare costs, whereas in reality, it has shrunk for that amount; conventional economists add healthcare costs to the GDP instead of deducting them.

Providing healthcare to everyone is so complicated and difficult that only 32 of the 33 most developed countries have figured it out! The 33rd is America, of course, because here, healthcare is a profitable business while everywhere else, healthcare is a human right but devastating for the economy as a whole.

We know that America spends far more on healthcare than any other country, even though about 8% of Americans don't get any. The second highest-cost country is Germany, where everyone is covered, and costs are 40% less than in America.

When my book Vultures: Doctors, Lawyers, Hospitals and Insurance Companies, What's Wrong and What to do About It was published in 1990, U.S. healthcare costs were $666.2 billion ($1.5 trillion in 2023 dollars). Healthcare costs in 1990 were 11.1% of GDP and $6,202 (2023 dollars) per capita.

In 2023, healthcare costs were $4.7 trillion — $14,100 per capita (227% of 1990 costs), 17.2% of GDP (a 55% larger share of GDP than in 1990).

The problem is that we do not understand the economics behind healthcare costs and their effects on the economy.

A single-payer system is not expensive if it's done the right way.

What's expensive is our obsolete delivery system, our experts lacking understanding of economics, and the corrupt lawmakers who take the interests of all special interest groups into consideration rather than those of the people and the economy.

Worse: the experts have no clue about the use of productivity in the service sector, which could reduce the cost of healthcare between 30% and 50% by creating cost-cutting and productivity-inducing specialized clinics, dubbed "Super-Clinics"! These clinics would make quality healthcare affordable, and the quality in the service sector would rise as productivity increases.

Further, they do not take into consideration the effects of the rising "social" and "recurring" costs of healthcare on the economy, which is outrageous! Healthcare cost is nothing more than the worst social cost! Surprisingly, conventional economists add healthcare costs to the GDP instead of deducting them from the GDP, creating fake economic growth!

In addition, we would never be able to create competitive manufacturing facilities with low-cost labor countries if our healthcare costs, along with interest and energy, keep rising out of control or even get into the production process. The fact is that an increase in the costs of healthcare, energy, and interest compound throughout the stages of production, making it unnecessarily expensive.

The malaise of our economy is not limited to just the above three sectors. Here are a few more, although not all of them.

Financial Institutions

Financial institution models are corrupt and self-defeating to begin with because they all concentrate on charging interest, interests of all kinds. If they cannot find new ways of charging interest, they employ fees of all kinds. Bankers and financial institutions should ask themselves how much longer they can employ these unethical and dubious activities before they are saturated and they are bankrupt. We must understand this simple reality: Money is the Oxygen of an economy. If there's a shortage of it in an economy, that economy will suffer shortness of breath. If it becomes too much, it burns the economy.

Interest is the Carbon Dioxide of an economy. If interest is charged on borrowed monies, it'll cause shortness of breath for that economy—the higher the interest rates, the worse the shortness of breath, and it could even suffocate the economy, too.

Stock markets are based on exploitation and Ponzi Schemes of all kinds, no matter how one looks at it. An economy should never be treated as a casino, luring people to become rich by ripping off others. The sad reality is that a lot of people must lose for a few to win.

Military Industrial Complex

Military industrial complex must have new wars to exist and prosper; without periodic wars to start with production to replace and create new markets for their weapons, it would be the end of their existence.

Manufacturing underlies the same pressure just to exist, which can last only so long before new companies overtake them or kick them out of the business.

Justice System

Justice and the legal system demand more lawsuits for rising numbers of lawyers chasing new cases to exist and possibly prosper; justice is just another corrupt, wealth-transferring, and social-costs-inducing business entity that pulls down the economy. One must be naïve to believe that the justice system in the United States is honest and respected. When one gets deep into their practices, there's very little difference between the mullah's Islamic sharia laws and those being practiced by the lawyers in the United States, especially in states controlled by the Democrats. No wonder that money serves justice.

Innovation

The United States, once the center of innovation, research & development, manufacturing, and wealth-creating activities in the world, is now the center of wealth-transferring and poverty-inducing activities. To realize this fact, all you need is to watch TV, go to social media, and pay attention to the telephone calls you receive. Without exaggeration, 95% of the advertising is related to wealth-transferring activities, selling solar energy systems manufactured in China at no monthly payment but added to the property taxes for the rest of your life; promoting benefits associated with social security, deceptive insurance policies, and the list goes on without any wealth-creating activities project.

Media

Generally, all regular and social media follow the same strategy: create controversy between their viewers and their competitors to generate income, publish advertising and promote write-ups for those who pay them for it, and join those candidates who generate or are supported with the most donations. Of course, to create controversy, they must take sides with the ruling political parties. If one expects to get any kind of unbiased and honest evaluation of the situation, that person must be dreaming or be very naïve. It must also be emphasized that expecting pure truth, unbiased information, and fact-checking from the writers of those media or other sources cannot be acceptable because one does not know about the level of knowledge, impartiality, and objectivity of the fact-checkers.

Consequently, the media is just another big source of rising and devastating social costs of all kinds because masses of people get instigated to get involved in potentially destructive, harmful, and violent activities. The best examples were the role of Iranian media before the downfall of the late Shah of Iran and the rise of the barbaric, terroristic mullah regime of the Islamic Republic of Iran in 1979 with the lunatic Ayatollah Ruhullah Khomeini. Also, it is not too distant past that the Americans could have forgotten the Democrats' insane and demented leadership activities against President Donald J. Trump, which were and still are a series of vicious, brutal, and dangerous chicaneries and deviousness.

These sample examples demonstrate that our business models are simply not based on wealth-creating activities. Instead, they encourage businesses to be the sources of destruction and rising social costs of all kinds.

It's no wonder that a great nation like the United States of America is in decline, going backward and downward to become a Third World country; these devastating trends must be stopped and reversed before it's too late. Once the flaws and shortcomings of conventional economics are clearly understood, implementation of their solutions is just a matter of political will and decision.

Imperative for All Economists to Understand these Realities

To make the failures of the above business approaches even clearer, below is explained more:

Gross Domestic Product

Gross Domestic Product (GDP): Any wealth-transferring activities or transactions that do not create new wealth or reduce recurring costs and/or social costs associated with people's living standards. It does not increase wealth in an economy; it only transfers wealth. Wealth-transferring activities enrich a person or a group at the expense of another person or group; neither new wealth is created, nor the economy becomes wealthier; if anything else other than that should happen, it is that the economy becomes only poorer due to the cost involved in wealth-transferring activities.

Maximizing Profits

Maximizing the profits is the most vicious, corrupt, and short-sighted approach. Why should anybody do all the right things and hard work when often all the wrong things can make achieving the goal much easier and faster in a shorter period, but if it continues, it'll take the economy to the brink of destruction.

Fees, Fines, Tolls And Interest

Measures such as fees, fines, tolls, and interest that chip away at the disposable income of regular people and small businesses dismantle a solid and vibrant economy. Similarly, governments that finance their expenditures with these sources of revenue gain are nothing other than chopping the roots of that economy with axes.

Size Of Government

Smaller government should not be the issue. We must have a competent and qualified government, which can only be realized by experts in the related fields who have coherent and comprehensive plans and a series of other qualifying features before a government can become useful and effective. Reducing a government from one hundred "Joe Biden's" and "Kamala Harris's" to only one "Joe Biden" and "Kamala Harris" will not make that administration any better or more effective either!

Transition Period

How can anybody "Build Back Better" when the first step that person, upon his arrival in the White House, takes is to implement an inept and stupid policy that triggers the rise of the gasoline and energy prices just to demonstrate his pertinacity to the sound policy of his predecessor? Energy is the elixir of an economy. Economies with lower energy prices have a big advantage over economies with higher energy prices, assuming all other factors remain the same. Any change in any sector of the economy necessitates the consideration of the associated transition period that comes with it to prevent the disturbance of that sector.

Inter-Relationship Of Economic Factors

The main shortcomings and failure of conventional economics are reflected in their inability to envision with some certainty the potential final outcomes of all different implemented approaches due to a lack of knowledge and understanding of the interactions, interconnection, and interdependence of all economic factors with each other, individually and combined with several economic factors due to their piecemeal approaches and practically zero knowledge of handling of and complete and total approach to an economy. It's like one hand does not know what the other hand is doing! It must be emphasized this shortcoming has nothing to do with the planned economies of the socialist and communist nations. We must have an economic plan for the different areas of an economy, which requires the knowledge to combine different economic factors to enable people to realize for themselves a decent, economic-environmentally sustainable, and lasting living standard.

An economic plan is totally different from a planned economy.

Austerity

Austerity is a confused approach. When an economy needs to deal with its recurring and social costs of all kinds, the last step is to tighten the belt. When a vehicle is about to run out of gasoline, the last measure you take is not to pump more gasoline in it to prevent it from coming to a final stop; you must fill the tank with more gasoline to move forward instead of coming to a stillstand. However, we must find ways to reduce and possibly eliminate the unnecessary recurring costs associated with it so as not to stop the vehicle from moving forward.

Trickle-Down Economic

Trickle-Down-Economic makes more sense from the business viewpoint than as an economic approach in an economy. The late famous radio anchor Rush Limbach described the Trickle-Down-Economic as follows: "When an owner of a gas station hires a few people to work at his gas station, the salary which he pays them from the revenue generated from the gas station trickles down to his workers and welfare of their families." This is a business approach, not an economic approach, even if it affects the standard of living of his employees because it is not a secured income, which could have a lasting effect until the end of the life of those employees. The effects are only temporary.

Solution to Interest

Unlike conventional economics, which finds a correlation between unemployment and inflation (Philips-Curve), in Zero Cost Economics, not only do interrelationships and interconnection between all economic factors exist, but they can be simple, complex, and/or combined with multiple economic factors leading to different outcomes. This reality must be learned and implemented to achieve the desired outcomes.

To remind it, if, in fact, there is a strong correlation between "unemployment" and "inflation" (as inflation goes up, unemployment goes down and vice versa) as the FED propagates, it means that they keep shoving a permanent "see-sawing" economy down our throats—a very worrisome concept for the people to have to depend on such an economy. How can such an economy ever be balanced? By cuts and layoffs, it's a totally inept and insane measure.

Raising interest rates to fight inflation is like using gasoline to fight fire, which burns down the demand until the lack of demand lowers inflation. That means more unemployment. It's not too smart to do it when better and more effective ways exist.

To make the finance world and people prosperous without causing inflation and debts, borrowed money should not be penalized with interest. Instead, deposits should be rewarded with relatively high interest. The trick to making it work lies in speeding up the velocity of return on investment. This requires an overhaul of the lending process. Profits made through this process can exceed figures unimaginable in the current finance world, which is governed by absurd and inept conventional lending practices and systems.

Healthcare

To remind you, healthcare costs are a very crucial factor in an economy, which conventional economics have failed miserably to understand. No matter how one looks at it, healthcare is a major social cost in an economy that must be eliminated. It's unfortunate that economists consider healthcare costs as a main post for economic growth. Instead of deducting it, they add it to the GDP. Healthcare costs are one of the biggest and the worst social costs in an economy, and they must be deducted instead of being added to GDP.

The second problem is that healthcare costs, like energy and interest, compound throughout the stages of production.

The third challenge is that healthcare must be provided to all people to prevent the potential costs associated with the absence of the workforce from their work due to their ailments, which has a negative effect on the performance and revenue of the company and the economy.

The fourth and biggest challenge that healthcare poses is that it cannot be resolved with money but with increased productivity, which conventional economics lack the definition of productivity in the service sector. A healthcare system that is improved and reformed (from the standpoint of cost) will enable us all to live a healthier life and contribute more to a vibrant, cost-effective economy. The key to it is to increase productivity, an area of economics that has yet to pique much interest, and it must be reformed.

Converting healthcare from being the largest source of social costs to the greatest source of creating wealth, making life for everybody enjoyable, and providing a long life to everybody is the lack of understanding of healthcare by all the experts.

To make it clear, healthcare comes in three types:

1) Curative medicine, which cures an ailment without fixing it. This type of medicine causes social costs of all kinds, which must be eliminated totally.

2) Preventive medicine, which is less costly than the former but still costs not as much as curative medicine, fails to keep one healthy forever to improve the quality of life and performance of a person until one is alive.

3) Perfective medicine in whichever forms, such as Quantum Medicine, Stem Cell Therapy or Herbal Medicine, and many other unknown discoveries, are challenges that we must strive for, which improves the health condition to the perfect condition and keeps it that way until one drops dead because of the physically reached limits. Alsheimer, Parkinson's, old age

symptoms of falling, prostate enlargement, impotency, and all other ailments should also become a matter of the past.

Additionally, it should get into the new era of improving people's defective organs; if they were born blind or were without a limp, etc., it could be improved by the improvement of medicine, which enables that person to enjoy life and be more productive. This is not utopian medicine; if we release ourselves from the greed and corruption that are caused by maximizing profits to an era much greater than anybody has ever imagined, we could achieve this goal. Our current way of thinking about medicine is so primitive to use it as a tool for maximizing profits instead of exploring the world beyond it in the perfect medicine and all the great things that may come with it for all of us—a whole world of unparallel health, happiness, and enjoyment ever seen or experienced by anyone in the past.

Realistically considered, it would be like a miracle, much bigger and greater than anything anybody ever did in the history of mankind, but also, economically, it would come with no less miracle, converting the largest recurring and escalating social costs to the biggest source of wealth-creation—what anything else could match this great achievement?! Certainly, hundreds of billions of dollars made by Pfizer and Moderna to vaccinate fearful COVID-19 people will be considered as one of the shameful mankind activities in comparison to this great opportunity.

To complement the economic thoughts behind healthcare issues requires reminding of a few earlier aspects of healthcare; conventional economists and politicians must understand and stop inept and wrong practices of the past, which are:

- Adding up healthcare costs to the Gross Domestic Product (GDP) instead of deducting it from the GDP.

- Realizing that an increase in healthcare costs compounds throughout the different stages of production, making it only expensive and uncompetitive with products manufactured in low-labor-cost nations as mentioned above.

Healthcare is the worst type of social cost that keeps recurring and rising, requiring all efforts to reduce it or, at best, eliminate it if we want healthcare for all people and, at the same time, a flourishing and competitive manufacturing facility in the U.S.

In plain English, to create a wealth-generating, vibrant, and healthy economy, all efforts must be made to reduce healthcare costs to a minimum level and, at best, eliminate the need for Curative and Preventive Medicine with Perfective Medicine, converting social costs caused by Curative and Preventive Medicine to Social Benefits by promoting Perfective Medicine.

In addition, much bigger efforts must be undertaken so that healthcare costs do not find their way into the production process, much less end up going through the different stages due to its compounding nature, as mentioned above.

The more a product must go through different stages of production, the more it compounds and the higher gets the cost of production.

Healthcare costs have a very direct correlation with manufacturing! In fact, if the cost of healthcare is not tamed nor eliminated, the only sure thing would be the collapse of the economy due to the unstoppable rising cost of healthcare or the decreasing access to healthcare. Conversely, the fastest way to a vibrant economy based on manufacturing would be the elimination of healthcare costs altogether.

The ignorance of economists and politicians goes even beyond that!

In 2023, the U.S. Gross Domestic Product (GDP) was only $27.36 Trillion.

In the same year (2023), the U.S. Healthcare costs were $4.80 Trillion.

No matter how one looks at it, healthcare costs are a social cost and inflationary.

Therefore, we must deduct $4.80 Trillion (twice the amount of healthcare cost, $4.80 X 2 = $8.16 Trillion for 2023) from the U.S. GDP of $27.36 Trillion in 2023, which brings down the GDP to $19.20 Trillion instead of $27.36 Trillion that the economists erroneously believe the GDP to be!

The reason for deducting healthcare costs two times the amount of $4.80 trillion from the GDP is that one time, it was wrongly added to the GDP, and the second, $4.80 trillion, which should have been deducted from the GDP in the first place. Many other social costs, such as maintenance costs, Food stamps, military, etc., have also been erroneously added to the GDP, which must be deducted from it, not only once, but twice for the same reason explained above, which would reduce the U.S. GDP even more.

The solution to U.S. healthcare and the economy requires an understanding of the problems involved in the first place, which, amazingly, nobody even knows what those problems are!

Worse: when politics, dogmas, greed, favoritism, corruption, etc., find the front seats, prudent and effective economics must take the back seat. It makes no difference whether economists are no better than others due to their lack of understanding of economics or they are guided by the same motives as the others!

Economy

In contrast to the popular opinion that our present political system is not based on the principles of democracy; actually, it is, which is the rule of the majority on the minority instead.

However, that majority is controlled by a group of plutocrats, a political system indirectly governed by a relatively small group of the rich and superrich, whom I call elite capitalists. Their foundation can be traced back to the profit-maximizing drive. This drive is the most devilish one, as was often mentioned earlier.

The business mindset that anything can be bought with money does not work in an economy.

"An economy cannot be bought; it must be built."

For an economy to increasingly rely on "recurring revenue" and rising "social costs" will only lead to failure and growing poverty in that economy! Conversely, rising revenue generated through new sources of revenue and decreasing social costs prove that the economy is getting robust, creating wealth, and becoming monetarily stable.

Maximizing the profit goal of businesses, if achieved through increased "recurring revenue" without creating new sources of revenue, would reach its limits sooner rather than later.

Similarly, any effort to generate more revenue unethically by manipulations and exploitation (such as fees, late fees, high interest rates, and trailing interest) to boost recurring revenue to secure the previous year's income level in real terms would only exacerbate the situation and lead to a permanent decrease of revenue in real terms unless "new sources of revenue" are found, and new revenues are generated.

In other words, new sources of revenue are less inflationary because it is generated through new innovations and products; no past results exist about them to require some sort of manipulation to achieve the same income level in real terms compared to the last one. The indisputable fact is that to reach an income level in the real term that is as high as the previous year through recurring revenues relying on old and obsolete products and services it requires to employ unethical and exploitative methods unless that product or service cannot satisfy the demand.

It is absurd to believe a currency backed by gold can be strong and stable without realizing it's not gold; it's the vibrant economy in which general prosperity is enjoyed at the lowest recurring costs and social cost of all kinds, which makes a currency stable, strong, and convertible. A flourishing economy with a strong manufacturing base and the lowest social costs of all kinds compared to other currencies can make the currency of that nation also a reserve currency.

The stability and convertibility of a currency do not depend on the GDP as the BRICS-Nations think; backing it with all the Gold in the World will help them very little, and boosting the military does not help a currency when it lacks a series of other needed features such as economic stability of the economy, economic freedom, and most importantly, low, or even the best, no social costs, much less rising social costs of all kinds with declining living standard of people of that economy. In other words, the more people in an economy keep enjoying a given living standard compared to the rest of the economies of the world with the lowest social costs per person, the currency of that country will start moving toward becoming strong, stable, convertible, and eventually be stored as a reserve currency.

A true economist must be equipped with all the knowledge that is involved in an economy, not in businesses only, which includes all the different factors of an economy. He or she must understand the interdependency, interconnection, and interrelationship between all the existing factors with each other, one with another individually, and several factors involved in a given situation with each other.

The most complicated ones are those when technological issues such as energy, environment, technology, innovation, natural disasters, distribution of income and wealth, and the like must be dealt with from political, legal, corruption, religious, and social issues aspects, especially by unqualified and incompetent people, whether they are billionaires, lawyers, businessmen, politicians, thugs, dictators (religious, military, civil or any other forms of it), who all are mainly driven by acquiring power and wealth to control the income and wealth which are anti-economy, anti- general prosperity.

Similarly, conventional dogmas also do not work in an economy to yield positive results, no matter how often they are tried or positive results are attributed to them. However, the best recipe for the annihilation of mankind is that we continue the conventional routes we are on. We must always remind ourselves that all people do what they have learned or know to do.

It does not mean that when they are put in a position, especially in an important one, they are simply qualified and competent for the job! They are not.

To be clearer: For instance, the current U.S. Treasury, Secretary Janet Yellen, a former Chairman of the Federal Reserve System, and a famous and distinguished economic professor at prestigious universities such as Harvard, The London School of Economics, and the University of California at Berkeley, a Keynesian economist, failed to understand how an economy works when the guideline is based on useless and flawed Keynesian Economic Theories. Replacing her with a professional lawyer and brilliant stock market specialist, Jerome Powell does not make anything better. Because one was a great professor who taught Keynesian economics, or the other was successful in the stock market, does not mean they are qualified for the job. I repeat: one must be an expert in that field and have a detailed spelled-out plan for the office to which he or she is being appointed. Otherwise, that move must be questioned.

How could those who appoint someone to a certain office be qualified to make that decision? Similarly, appointing a certain number of people from different races, genders, and sexual orientations in an administration for political gains and votes is equally questionable and absurd.

How insecure living in the United States has become with Kamala Harris? It must be a nightmare for all Americans to imagine that Kamala Harris can become president in the next election! You cannot run a nation like the United States with grating "laughs!" We have a serious problem; we must make the right choices. Remember:

"All people do what they have learned or know to do."

To emphasize something that cannot be emphasized enough!

Similarly, conventional economists are not economists; they all are business administrators who didn't learn or understand that business measures are the wrong ones to run an economy; they'll always fail because they all are ill-equipped, wrong, and anti-economy when maximizing profits is their driving goal.

Incompetency and lack of qualification for any job, including for a governmental office, cannot be helped even if the person is inexperienced in that field, even if that person is a "billionaire" and has the highest university degree in an unrelated area.

Wealth-creating jobs, not wealth-transferring transactions, lead to non-inflationary, general prosperity in an economy.

We must employ effective and useful economic measures to run an economy, enabling us to realize general property with economic-financial security for all people.

Only Zerocrats, a group of qualified, competent, patriotic, and honest experts from different fields with a deep understanding of Zero Cost Economics, can shape a peaceful and prosperous future for all—not Democrats, Rinos, conventional economists, and politicians, as well as billionaires.

The Cost of Ignorance – Food for Thoughts

Unfortunately, everything in life comes with more costs than benefits. However, ignorance comes with the highest cost. Here are some examples of real-life situations as "food for thoughts:"

- We often hear who controls debt, controls everything. But how much value do indebted people have, especially when you have robbed them naked, and there's no prospect of robbing them anymore? What's left there to be controlled?

- Donate to us, and you can deduct it from your taxes. But how do you deduct from your taxes when you have no income to have taxes paid to be able to deduct from your taxes?

- When you hire unemployed people, politicians promise to give you a $3,000.00 tax credit for every new hire. Why would anyone spend $30,000.00 to hire somebody just to collect a $3,000.00 tax credit, especially when the business is on the nosedive? When the business is doing well, one hires the people needed regardless of tax incentives.

- Many businesses tell their clients that they will not increase their monthly payments, but after a while, the monthly rates keep increasing incrementally. Cheating and fleecing have become a normal business practice and a source of generating windfall revenue.

- When we switch our service from one outfit to another to lower our monthly payment, we often get quotes that are lower than those of the previous company, but the new company hardly confirms it in writing. A month later the big surprise arrives with the first statement.

- More and more restaurants state at the bottom of the credit card slips the amount of different percentages of tips to save the customers from having to calculate the amount of tip to add to the amount of the statement. Many restaurants add tips on the amount of tax as well, which they put in their pockets.

- Hospitals and clinics have no price list for their services, and they expect that their bill will get paid, especially when you do not have insurance. Try going to a restaurant that has no price printed on their menu. You'll end up regretting having eaten that food there.

- Why would anybody vote a second time for a failed politician? How could anybody expect a better performance from that person the second time? If s/he could have done it, s/he would have done it in the first place.

- I got this text message from HMP, a Democratic PAC, which described themselves to be committed to defeating radical Republicans and winning back the House Majority:
    - "Before Kamala's speech: Dems get a(n) 800% MATCHED donation (highest ever)"
    - $5 = $45; $10 = $90; $25 = $225
    - Does it make sense to anybody? Why does somebody have to donate $5 for them to get $45, $90, and $225? Why don't they ask the generous donor to donate $45, $90, $225, and be done with it. Building a foundation on stupidity will never be strong and solid.

Time to smart up! Don't let others treat you as being an unintelligent person.

Why Zero Cost Economics is the Answer—Reasons, Approaches, and Backgrounds?

Due to the nature of the economic problems, they all are mainly escalating and accelerating social costs of all kinds, which are caused by social, religious, and legal issues as well as by the drive to maximize profits by the businesses reflected in inflation, unemployment, immigration, lack of affordability to eat and live, rising energy costs, lack of healthcare, low-pay, housing, financial insecurity, crime, and the list goes on and on.

When we have a prudent and effective economic concept to follow and have coherent and comprehensive economic-monetary plans to implement, not only will the economy flourish and become vibrant, but also the businesses will undergo the same positive changes. They start to prosper without the need to maximize profit. However, if we continue to strive toward maximizing the profits' goal, the economy will collapse. Instead, the legal system – the biggest source of social costs of all kinds and corruption - will prosper. The last thing we want to create in the United States of America is to end up becoming like the Islamic Republic of Iran (IRI).

Whether we like it or not, the United States is already on the path to becoming just like the Islamic Republic of Iran. In IRI, we have "Ayat-Ollahs"; we don't want the United States to be ruled by such dubious and questionable attorney generals such as "Merrick Garland-Ollah," "Laticia James-Ollah," "Alvin Bragg-Ollah," and "Fani Willis-Ollah," or by judges such as "Juan Merchan-Ollah, and "Arthur Ergoron-Ollah."

They both follow the laws: The former follows the "divine" laws; the latter all kinds of fuzzy laws; neither one of the groups follows the laws that provide justice.

Therefore, religion and the legal profession must be "de-politized;" these two groups must be kept away from getting involved in any kind of political process if they are involved in religion and the legal profession. No country in the world, much less the United States, should ever end up like the Islamic Republic of Iran and Afghanistan. In other words: Religion and legal profession should be banned from politics and as politicians. Otherwise, it would be just like the mullahs in Iran and the Taliban in Afghanistan, two religious groups ruling the country to ruins. Law and religion are not only anti-economy, but they are harmful and devastating, as we have seen in the Islamic of Iran and Afghanistan, and most recently, the past 8 years (2016 – 2024) are witnessing it in the United States with all the indictments, prosecutions, and weird judgments.

As we know by now and have been experiencing it for ages, conventional economics are inflationary and debt-inducing, which affects people in a devastating way.

The difference between the two conventional economic systems is:

The Capitalistic Economic Model serves only 1% of the rich and super-rich; 99% of people end up living in rising poverty and destitution.

The Socialistic Economic Model is simply poverty-inducing.

Consequently, neither one of these two economic models will ever be able to serve most of the people, much less all people.

We all must also understand this reality, not live with the illusion of becoming rich one day but ending up living in poverty until the day we die.

If the common relationship between rich and poor is what is known to be as 99% (poor) to 1% (rich), then we should seriously think of our chances to become rich one day by blowing away other, more realistic options. We should think about the following seriously.

Assuming that for:

- 1% of people want to become rich, 99% of people must work one shift.
- 2% of people want to become rich, 98% of people must work two shifts.
- 3% of people want to become rich, 97% of people must work three shifts.

It makes it clear that, at best, no more than 3% of the population of a normal economy can ever become rich. Therefore, it should not be a goal to pursue because of the rising insecurity expected during old age. However, by implementing the Zero Cost Economy model, lasting prosperity and economic-financial security can be realized for all people, which will not cost; it pays. This is possible if we implement prudent and effective economic-monetary policies that can convert the rising social costs of all kinds associated with an insecure existence to a decent, secure living standard for all people. After that transition period, most of those social costs, if not all of them, are no longer needed and gone. Consequently, not only does it not cost, but it also pays.

Another negative phenomenon of conventional economics is the "boom and bust" that happens so often, which an economy should never go through in the first place. Instead of providing a constantly rising general prosperity and economic-financial security, conventional economics send growing numbers of people to poor houses and to an insecure future, especially when people expect to retire and enjoy the remaining of their life in peace and economic-financial security.

This all is absurd and does not need to be the case if we could just understand how an economy works and how to handle it, which is described in Zero Cost Economics.

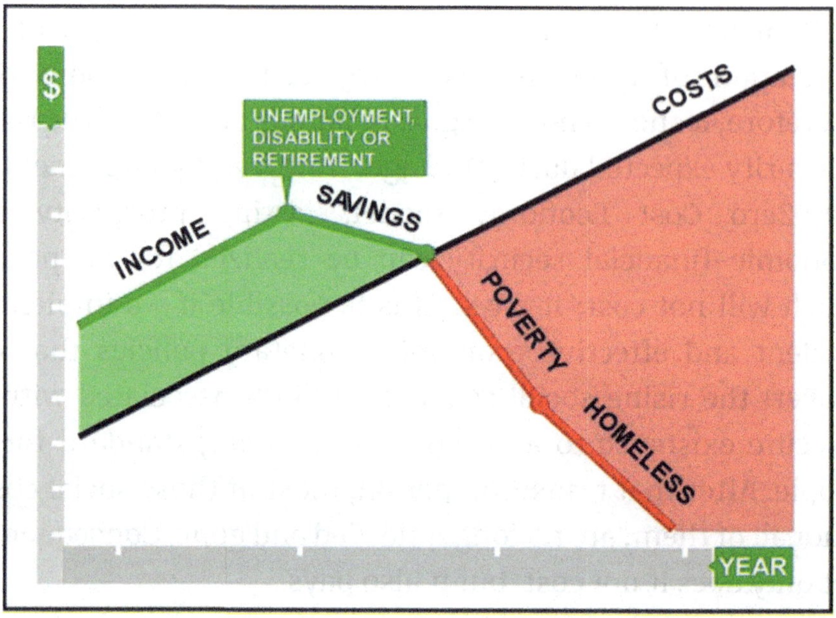

What really makes conventional economics fail – as explained earlier – are the recurring costs and social costs of all kinds, especially associated with people's standard of living and lack of economic-financial security for the masses of people.

To be more precise, the immediate and much bigger threat than the rising National Debts to the U.S. Economy and the National Security are the rising regular Recurring Costs and Recurring Social Costs of all kinds, which are associated with maintaining as well as declining people's standard of living. Certainly, the de-dollarization attempts of the BRICS Nations will not make combating the related challenges any easier, although for now, it is an additional unwanted and unwelcome challenge added to the U.S. economy.

The reason for this assertion is that the rising regular "Recurring Costs" and "Recurring Social Costs" of all kinds pose a much higher and immediate threat to the National Security of the United States than the National Debts; it can be triggered by recurring costs and social costs of all kinds. These are caused by housing (rent and mortgage), unemployment, energy (gasoline, electricity), healthcare, food, taxes, insurance (natural disasters, healthcare, accidents, sudden death), interest, small businesses, poverty, homeless, education, innovation, entrepreneurship, regulations, and the list go on. Now, the influx of some twelve to fifteen million unvetted and illegal immigrants does not help the existing complex and critical situation. If all of it was done to influence the election results, it would be the ineptest and stupidest step ever taken for anything by anybody, assuming the election outcome was in their favor—all they achieved would be problems over problems to deal with.

These facts make it clear to everybody: to create a great economy, we must implement prudent and effective economic-monetary policies that make it possible to have a decent and acceptable living standard for all people, ensuring everybody has an enjoyable and secure standard of living. Further, we must strive to make sure that our net national revenues, in real terms, keep exceeding our costs of all kinds.

(Note: To be very clear, it means that national revenues should be without inflation and debts, not like the conventional way of calculating it.

To make it clearer, assuming our National Revenue in 2023 was $100 Billion in real terms without inflation and potential debts, at ZERO inflation rate, in 2024, at least our National Revenue should be $100 Billion. In conventional economics, it must be $110 Billion, assuming the inflation rate was 10%. Of course, it may never happen, but that should be the goal.)

Even though running an economy is much different than a private household, there are some similarities between them. It is not difficult to imagine that a nation like a private household would be in good shape when everything that it needs has been acquired and paid for and live without any debt other than the daily expenses for food and other periodic expenses without having any regular recurring costs. In this case, that economy does not need too much income to pay for the maintenance costs for the achieved standard of living. Once this stage is reached, more and more people will not need to work as usual to meet ends. Reaching this stage, living expenses become a matter of the past. At this point, we enter a "Leisure Economy' which poses its own challenges. This is another subject which at this point is irrelevant to waste any time on it, but realizing such an economy is the stage to reach which would make all today's economic woes a matter of past, a real rewarding, and enjoyable life can be envisioned to become a reality for all people by eliminating all social costs of all kinds. However, it must be emphasized that reaching a Leisure Economy requires – in an ideal situation - that all people of that economy have a decent, acceptable standard of living without any recurring costs associated with that standard of living and without any social costs of any kind in that economy.

To achieve this goal, we must change the direction in which we were until now by abandoning a series of economically wrong approaches and replacing them with a series of new and right ones, some of which are as follows:

Businesses and government agencies must abolish maximizing profit driven by replacing it with "ethical" profits. It also includes distancing from all kinds of dubious activities such as looting, fleecing, and cheating customers and people by charging them interest, late fees, trailing interest, and overdraft fees; the list is endless. It should be clear to everybody that all these dubious activities are not only unfair and self-defeating, but they're also inflationary and debt-inducing. These are problems that we are facing increasingly and must be eliminated. By doing this, there will be no need for businesses to be driven by the goal of maximizing profits because – as mentioned earlier - the best guarantee for businesses to prosper is prosperous people in a vibrant economy. The reason: when people are not fleeced and looted, they will become prosperous and spend their money on businesses.

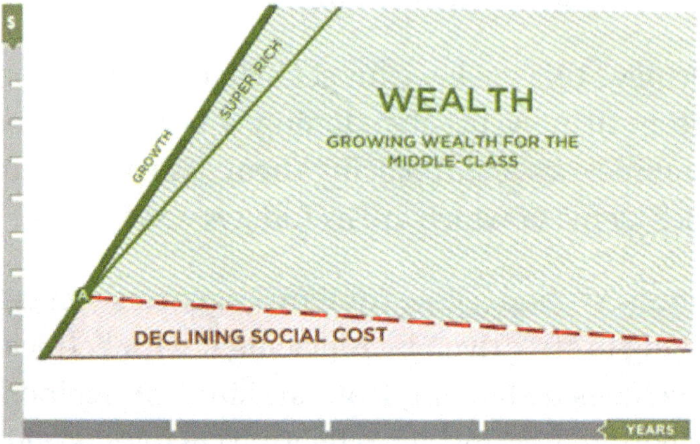

Economic Growth, wealth and social costs development based on the concetps of Zero Cost Economics. A Zero Cost Economy can be realized between 6 and 8 years.

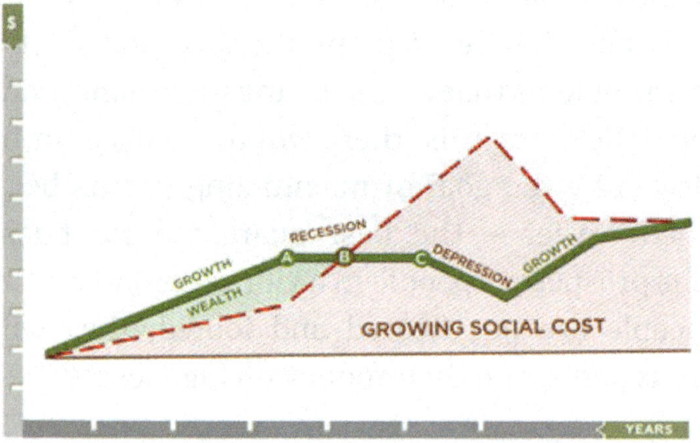

Economic Growth, wealth and social costs development based on the Conventional Economic models and implementing Gross Domestic Products (GDP) as the calculation method.

Note: the development of these three factors relates to their growth.

The yardstick to measure the performance of an economy must be changed from the Gross Domestic Product (GDP) to "Economic Security Indices (ESI)," which provide us with the exact changes that had taken place in terms of qualitative and qualitative growth of every item related to a general standard of living of people such as housing, education, healthcare, energy self-sufficiency, insurance coverage, small businesses, and destructive activities including destruction of wealth through natural disasters, etc.

All types of taxes and all income models must be abolished and replaced with "Prosperity-Inducing-Income (PII)," which is non-inflationary and non-debt-inducing. Instead, it's prosperity-inducing. This should replace all compensation methods, including pensions, social security, living wages, wages, salaries, etc. This measure will create tremendously more middle-class, reduce poverty to a minimum, and the one percent rich and super-rich will always be if they decide to hoard wealth and leave it for some stranger to spend after their death. In other words, wealth will lose its power to manipulate and influence politicians and politics to rule and exploit for temporary advantage at the expense of the majority. Although it will take the power from the rich and superrich to acquire political power, instead, it will enable everybody to live economically a better and more peaceful life, never possible under any form of conventional "elite" capitalistic or socialistic economic systems.

All types of compensations, salaries, wages, living wages, and incomes from all other sources are unfair, inflationary, debt-, and poverty-inducing, especially for the average working people except for those who are destined to become rich and superrich. As a result, these two factors cause the worst imbalance in any economy. And become the source of all the economic woes we are facing today, including the influx of some 15 million unvetted illegal immigrants to the United States.

Based on the definition of income, it must not cause inflation and debt for anybody. Instead, it must satisfy the need of the person, which is fair, sufficient, and prosperity-inducing for all people and the economy. To achieve this in an equitable economy, the highest earner in each economy should not take a maximum of ten times more than the lowest earners in that economy. Due to the fact that not all economies are equally prosperous; some are less prosperous, and others are much more prosperous, they all must be treated according to the standard in which they find themselves.

In should be reminded, should the Trump Campaign decide to demolish Joe Biden in the forthcoming presidential election, this would be, along with the housing projects, two unbeatable platforms that cannot be beaten even with all the cheatings, plots, and other dubious, crooked, and foul games that maybe in cooking. These goals can also be realized in real life without worries about their implementation.

Borrowed money should carry a zero-percent interest to avoid or keep it at a minimum from inducing inflation, debts, and poverty. Instead, we should reward deposits with relatively high interest rates to encourage people to deposit their savings in banks and financial institutions to avoid printing new money to prevent inflation. Zero-interest financing should be available for ready-to-go projects. The next step would be to fund the project with the expectation of increasing the velocity of return-on-investment. If done properly, the profits could reach a level that is unimaginable in today's practices by banks and financial institutions. The issues and approaches presented above, along with many other topics, are discussed in my forthcoming books.

Zero Cost Economics provides effective alternatives and solutions to reform conventional economies in almost all aspects of an economy in the interest of eliminating all the setbacks, failures, insecurities, and dark sides resulting from practicing conventional economics, either liberal or conservative models.

However, a short insight into a few topics may be inspiring:

It describes how, by having the banking and financial systems undergo rigorous and effective organizational and business changes and reform, they could make more "ethical" profits than ever. It is possible under conventional systems and practices. It would also spur non-inflationary and debt-free general prosperity for all people.

Implementation of "Zero Cost Cities" projects is another approach that will boost the housing market, skyrocketing the profits for financial institutions and lowering the prices of houses as new projects are built.

Economic plan is offered for stimulating and funding "Zero-cost enterprises" for talented entrepreneurs to revive the U.S. Economy to an unmatched standard in the world: unfortunately, the "Small Business Administration (SBA)" does not fulfill this requirement, which must be reformed.

There'll be a complete chart and guidelines of all the economic factors, their inter-relationship, inter-connections, and interdependency with each other. It will provide a useful tool for making economic and business decisions; it is high time to retire "Phillip-curve" as a tool to combat inflation and unemployment.

A word of wisdom:

When a person is in power and has all the possibilities and ability, s/he should shape the world in such a manner that afterward, when s/he is no longer in power, s/he can be able to live among the regular people and want to leave it for his/her children to live there too. Not to regret the missed opportunity. The legacy is the only thing that remains from a person after everything else is over. This opportunity should not be lost.

Why Social Costs Must be Converted to Social Profits and Social Benefits?

The main problem with all economies is that they are based on growing "social costs."

Social costs are inflationary, debt-inducing, and, consequently, diminish the purchasing power of the currency.

As mentioned earlier, an ideal condition for an economy is to have no social costs of any kind. At least, all efforts must be made to freeze and/or reduce the social costs of all kinds and then convert them to "social profits."

When "social costs" are eliminated, saved expenditures from the social costs become "social profits," which can be used to improve people's lives in that economy. In other words, a reduction and/or elimination of social costs become "social profits," which can be passed out as "social benefits" to people.

To create a prosperous economy, we must concentrate increasingly on "wealth-creating" and "recurring-cost-reducing" activities rather than on wealth-transferring activities. To remind you, wealth-transferring activities do not increase wealth, and often, they are either social costs or eventually lead to rising social costs of all kinds. On the other hand, any economic system that is based on growing social costs is not sustainable, and sooner or later, it will collapse. This is exactly what's happening right now with all the economies in the world, including those of the United States of America.

To turn around this dire situation, we must focus on eliminating our social costs of all kinds to enable us to increase our social benefits and pass them out.

In a nutshell, to increase social benefits, first, it must start with enforcing the use of increased productivity in manufacturing and service sectors by employing - in contrast to the conventional practices - a series of sound and prudent "economic-monetary" policies that can make possible an environmentally safe, sustainable, and lasting prosperity with economic-financial prosperity for all people of that economy; deficit-spending and handouts do not and cannot do it because they are the sources of rising social costs of all kinds.

To realize this goal, we must reform the banking and insurance industries rigorously and effectively to lower the compounding costs of interest and insurance during the stages of the production process, which would make insurance affordable and accessible for all people. Consequently, both industries will be making more profits just because of it.

On the other hand, converting the existing "social costs" into "social benefits" would not only reduce the costs of food and living but also create thousands of new jobs immediately.

These two plans would not cost a single additional penny to implement because we are already paying for them in terms of social costs (taxes) to the government directly and to the people indirectly.

We must keep in mind that in an oligopolistic and monopolistic economy, hardly any businesses, especially banking, financial institutions, insurance companies, and communications entities, can serve people and an economy fairly when they are driven by maximizing profit's goal.

It is also very important to pay attention to the fact that masses of people in no economy can ever enter the "Leisure Society" and enjoy it when they are haunted by regular recurring living costs, and its economy as a whole is suffering from rising social costs of all kinds.

What's needed to achieve these goals is know-how and leadership, which will be explored in detail in the forthcoming Parts 3 and 4 of this series of books.

"By converting social costs into social benefits, we can alleviate people's standard of living."

Time to Determine Our Own Future Wisely

Any election based on popular votes should not impress or excite anybody because it is not only the biggest swindle and deception in the world of politics but also the most inept and corrupt method of electing candidates because hardly qualified and competent candidates get elected. Similarly, don't be fooled by believing that the popular voting system is democracy in action.

The future and welfare of the people and nation is a serious and very important matter that cannot be decided by being promoted and hyped by the corrupt, biased, and hostile media, financed by special interest groups and greedy, power-hungry billionaires, endorsed by movie actors, followed by rhetoric of all kinds, celebrated as "democracy" being in action just to win the election.

When one takes a deeper look at how popular votes become the determining factor in any election, it becomes clear that no democracy is in play to reflect the real will of the people; democracy is nothing more than a smoke screen.

How could democracy exist under these conditions when:

1) Majority could be, in extreme cases, 50% plus one vote of the participating voters.

2) Rights of minorities suffer from just two votes less by getting 50% minus one vote.

3) Influence of money, political parties, and religious groups are anti-democracy forces that play major roles.

4) Fake news and lies by all types of media influence voters.

5) No funding and support from political parties and religious groups for independent but qualified and competent candidates exist.

6) No consideration is given to the qualification and competency of a candidate rather than the money he raised and whose endorsement he got.

7) No effective method of control exists to ensure votes are counted properly.

Further, relying on judgment and endorsements of questionable, dubious characters of certain politicians of both parties is certainly not a smart move, especially when all of them are lawyers, and all they know is indictments, impeachments, smear politics, and by getting their fake media propagandas to support them. In the past eight years, we had plenty of it, which would have destroyed any other country if it was not for the United States of America and former President Donald J. Trump's endurance and resistance.

Whether we have realized it or not, legal battles, in whichever form they take place, are pure and the worst sources of social costs of all kinds, which affect us all directly in our suffering from rising inflation and debts.

Fortunately, we witnessed and lived directly under the presidency of both administrations, Donald J. Trump and Biden-Harris Administration.

Despite all the dirt and accusations thrown toward former President Trump, including COVID-19, he ran the economy and national and international affairs of the United States in an optimum and flawless situation. No Monica Lewinsky affair or unkosher deals were made with any country in the world, the least with the Islamic Republic of Iran.

In contrast, the Joe Biden-Kamala Harris Administration treated the United States as a conquered nation and looted her directly or indirectly through the influx of illegal, unvetted immigrants, inflation, riots, incarceration of opposition, an embarrassing withdrawal from Afghanistan leaving over $80 billion military hardware for the Taliban, rising insecurity, crime, and poverty in the United States.

Just one point should be reminded to all Americans: if any of you are striving and dreaming to have a better standard of living, have a house, healthcare, more and cheaper food to fill your hungry stomach, not to become a victim of crime, have a secured retirement, or any other hope, you all must realize that some 12 to 15 million immigrants will be competing with you, or you have to stand in line with a stretch hand for your turn, which may never happen.

We must realize that the United States is not a stable and that anybody could just walk freely into this country, no matter who they were and for whatever reasons. They are coming here.

I must make it clear to every reader of this book: I have seen directly how it was done in the pre-Islamic Republic of Iran during the reign of the late Shah of Iran, which led to the downfall of the Shah of Iran and the rise of lunatic Ayatollah Ruhollah Khomeini, and the barbaric, terroristic Mullah-regime of the Islamic Republic of Iran, and for over 45 years of agony, poverty, and millions of deaths of the innocent Iranians.

Just to understand one feature of inflation and the diminishing purchasing power of currency, this example will make it very clear.

During the Shah, One U.S. dollar was equivalent to 7 Iranian Toman.

Today, One U.S. dollar is equivalent to 57,933.21 Iranian Toman.

That means, during the late Shah of Iran, nobody complained about hunger, lack of jobs, housing, education, healthcare, human rights, or equality between man and woman, but short after the notorious revolution, misery, suffering, hunger, homelessness, and death, execution has become a normal thing. People of Iran, who represent only one percent of the world's population but living in a country rich with nine percent of the world's precious raw material, must search for leftover food in people's dumpsters or sell one of their kidneys to feed themselves and their family—temporarily.

How did they get themselves in this dire and terrible situation? Because they fell into the trap of Ayatollah Khomeini's promise to give them free houses, free bus rides, and free electricity..., but they didn't even get a free death, like my father.

My father was executed for not denouncing his non-Muslim religion. After his execution, the Mullah regime charged my mother for the bullets with which they executed my father. And confiscated everything we had in that country.

Fortunately, there was still a free nation that welcomed us! Once the United States is gone, where do we go from here?!

All Americans must be warned, the playbook that the current Biden-Harris Administration has played for the past three and half years under the leadership of former President Barak Hussein Obama is to take over the United States politically and create a one-party system.

Remember these expressions of victory:

- Kamala Harris to Joe Biden: "Joe, we won!"
- Chuck Schumer: "When we win, we change America!"

We should all not let America get changed the way Barack Hussein Obama, Kamala Harris, and Chuck Schummer want. And let's not forget the misery that was brought upon Iranians, including my and other families in Iran, by a Democratic president, Jimmy Carter.

Now, what about the former President Donald J. Trump?

I must say if I were stuck in the middle of the ocean and about to be drowned, and there would come Donald Trump in a small boat to my rescue, and at the same, Kamala Harris would show up in a cruiser to my rescue, I would without any hesitation jump on Trump's boat.

I am confident that my chances of survival are much higher with Trump than with Harris.

You be the judge: Just ask yourself what did Kamala Harris perform in her entire life to get to this position in the first place? Certainly, not her intellect! No smart woman like the former Congresswoman Tulsi Gabbard would ever let that happen to her.

Now, we have her running mate the former Governor of Wisconsin, Tim Walz, not known to be any better than her.

Smart people do not become marionets of anybody.

When you ask Americans and foreigners for the reasons of not liking or hating President Donald J. Trump, often they mention he lies, he is bankrupted, he cheated, he is stupid, he lacks intellect, and he is not intelligent, and the likes. And when you ask them to give an example of their allegations and accusations, they fail to give one, or you hear all those you hear in the media.

But nobody ever used their own brain for a second to ask themselves a simple question—if the former President Trump were only one of the accusations or allegations which were made against him and would have been true, why would he be in this enviable position, loved by tens of millions of Americans, politicians and businessmen, and the list goes on until he ran for the office. Whatever President Donald Trump was, one thing is for sure--he was not stupid, which is often said about him. His interviews from his younger years are living proof of it, which were done on liberal media by liberal anchors.

The problem started with the former Donald J. Trump when he decided to challenge the political Swamp and the Globalists, an association of rotten looters whose existence was threatened.

Coming back to the choice between Donald J. Trump and Kamala Harris, which one should I vote for?

Here are your choices:

1) To vote for Donald J. Trump, who in November 2015 published his economic plan:

   Crippled America – How To Make America Great Again

Or for:

2) Kamala Harris, for her grating laughs and antics?

Apart from all these realities mentioned above, here are two simple questions that you must ask these two candidates:

a) What are you going to do for people like us and protect this great nation?

b) How are you going to do it?

Make your decision based on the answers to these two questions by comparing them with their records—both Trump and Harris have a record to compare.

Certainly, one move would be disastrous! Don't fall for empty promises like those of Ayatollah Khomeini to the brainless Iranians—you do not want to suffer the same fate! Instead of getting free houses, practically most of them ended up in graves, which were not even free. Families of the victims had to borrow money to bury their loved ones. When it comes to consolidating power, nothing hinders one from promising anything necessary until the goals are reached, but once supporters become disenchanted and start to protest, they are treated harshly—Ayatollah Khomeini and his successors sent them to the grave.

The rest you can forget!

It's all a smoke screen.

Think about your future, your family, and your children---and the United States of America!

The Road to the Future

The road to the future is divided in two contradicting directions:

1) The one we are already in the middle of, which will take us to an unknown, questionable, and terrible direction; and the other,

2) Toward a bright future.

Mankind has never achieved some kind of balance between anything they ever tried to realize or to take away from others simply because of perverse ideologies and drives, which were driven by greed to acquire power, wealth, and enjoy a lustful and lavish life, whether through religion, politics, military, or economic and financial manipulations and exploitation of the dependent and vulnerable people.

Killing, murdering, colonization, and wars were and are still tools to realize their goals if financial and economic manipulations and exploitation failed.

If the challenges with which the world was facing were still relatively small, and the losses and suffering were somehow either controllable or could not be seen by the world population, or hardly anybody could not have noticed what was going on or happened a thousand miles away from them, it would have been at least something that would not have captivated world's people attention. Today, the challenges are totally different, and the ineptness and incompetence of the rulers and leaders of the world have exceeded those of any generation before without realizing that their duty is to serve the people, not by exploiting them, get themselves enriched, and plot to ensure that it last for as long as they are alive. This does not end here; they want to pass on to their children and their children's children, too.

That's nothing new anyway; kings always did it. Now, the religious and political parties' leadership does too. Mullahs in the Islamic Republic of Iran, Taliban in Afghanistan, Communist and Socialistic parties in China, Russia, Cuba, and Venezuela, and in the United States, the Democrat Party.

Democrat Party changed with the former President Jimmy Carter and his young advisor, Senator Joe Biden. Democrat Party went through an upheaval, especially later with the Clintons, but a young, cunning Barak Hussein Obama came out of nowhere to become the U.S. president. Some Black and even White Americans see him as a God-given gift but do not realize how a U.S. president with a total salary of $2.8 million in eight years of his presidency can buy a few mansions for each $14 to $16 million. From book sales, such amounts cannot be earned to pay those kinds of amounts.

After Barack Obama's presidency, the plot for dominance of the political arena started through the Democratic Party to take over the United States; the dice fell on Joe Biden and Kamala Harris, the two smartest marionets of the Democrats of recent years.

Now, the United States is at the crossroads between choosing to be a free nation or to join the model of the Islamic Republic of Iran, Cuba, Venezuela, and the rest from where all the people still escape to the United States.

In this connection, it is necessary to remind all Americans that the leadership of the Democratic Party is the lackeys of the United Kingdom, Globalists, George Soros, Hollywood actors, Social Media giants, and many of the unconscious Billionaires and economists who have no clue what an economy is as it was explained in the book.

Unfortunately, the Democrats are not the only threat posing to the United States' freedom and prosperity—there are other enemies that must be dealt with.

1) The World Economic Forum, in Davos, Switzerland, with its founder Klaus Schwab, who plots to globalize the World. Is one of them. Just to give you a taste of what's in the pipeline for you, me, and others, just listen to this statement of him: "You'll own nothing, but you'll be happy!" This is the new definition of happiness.

2) Nobody knows for sure whether we, the people, will be happier with Klaus Schwab or with Blackrock, State Street, and Vanguard, which own 88% of the S&P 500, practically everything. They are buying every house they can, and rent it back to us? Not too difficult what that means!

3) The third group that has put its eyes on the United States is the United Kingdom by creating a non-profit organization advocating closer trade and diplomatic ties between, Canada, Australia, New Zealand, and the United Kingdom, dubbed CANZUK International. Knowing how Britain's political machinery think, they need a strong military power to be under their control with Democrats in power; the MAGA movement since President Donald J. Trump it doesn't seem to be a conspiracy theory anymore.

If anybody should wonder why President Donald J. Trump, once the darling of the Democrats and Republicans, is suddenly being hated like a pest, all he or she needs to do is to go to these three groups and do some deeper research and their ties to the Democrats. Also, one should listen to Trump's speech at the United Nations challenging the Globalists.

The other road to the future is that we make prudent and smart decisions in favor of all American people and The United States of America. Because we cannot prefer those non-American citizens, the unvetted, illegal immigrants over our own suffering people, who practically invaded our nations without following and respecting our nations and the laws of our nation. Most importantly, we have plenty of needy Americans, especially among the Democrats, Blacks, Whites, Spanish, and other races who are more in need of our help and have priority over the illegal immigrants.

First and foremost, we must help our own people, before we can help others; as the famous proverb says, charity starts at home.

How our future will look depends on which direction we decide to go at this juncture! Should we think that our progress has reached its maximum level and ends up here and decide for it, undoubtedly, we will increasingly become economically and financially slaves of the ruling class for as long as we live.

An economy underlies permanent dynamic processes, one of which is what we all decide. On the other hand, sooner or later, certain developments, good or bad, will take place, which will shape the "Leisure Society" by developing and employing "Artificial Intelligence (AI)" in almost every area of our lives.

As soon as this happens, development will take shape in areas that we cannot imagine today, or it may sound like science fiction to you. I don't want to take away anything from my forthcoming books which deal with these questions from economic and business standpoints, but I can tell you with full confidence that the role of money, wealth, becoming rich and superrich, having several mansions like Obama's, Bezos's, Gates's, and the likes will be a matter of past. As evolution and developments take shape, people will find there's so much more to discover and enjoy that they'll feel that their normal life is too short to chase those priorities that we chase today.

Cryptocurrency is another area where we know very little about how to use it. Today, whichever way we employ it, it cannot escape these two negative realities:

1) It's a Ponzi scheme and will collapse sooner or later, or

2) It can be employed to control people and their behaviors for political seasons, as the Democrats, World Economic Forum, and our friends at Blackrock, State Street, and Vanguard are planning to do or may end up doing it.

But AI, cryptocurrency, and many other future developments can be like guns and bullets—it can be used to kill enemies, such as your poverty, or kill you, your bright future.

When I ran for Florida governor in 2010, I wanted to create a publicly owned bank called The Bank of the State of Florida, employing the same "Fraction Reserve Regulation" that all regular banks use for their own benefits. I wanted to use it to benefit all Floridians by freeing them from paying all kinds of taxes that are levied on them.

Of course, it was a lost opportunity for the people of Florida and a big disappointment for me because I didn't get elected; I was not supported by the media because Big Money didn't support me. On the other hand, I would also not have taken money from them, anyway. In my forthcoming book, Liberal Dystopia, I discuss it in detail about it.

Exactly fourteen (14) years later, Florida Chief Financial Officer (CFO) Jimmy Patronis proposed the "Sunshine Freedom

Bank," a public bank of Florida that would establish state control over state funds. Whether it will go as far as I wanted to take the Florida State Bank to benefit the people is a question that the future will decide. However, this much I can say with certainty: no economic and financial project in an economy can succeed without being built on the foundation of Zero Cost Economics and focusing on freezing, reducing, and/or eliminating regular recurring costs and the rising social costs of all kinds which haunt the economy. Creating a state bank does not lead to success unless you deal with both types of costs: regular recurring costs and social costs of all kinds.

Today, 14 years have passed, Florida State Bank may or may not become successful, but by combining cryptocurrency and AI with Zero Cost Economics, it offers a great and endless opportunity much bigger than the state bank or any project can provide—the road to the future must go through cryptocurrency, AI combined with the Zero Cost Economics.

The rest of the plans in the pipeline are just unrealistic and pipedreams.

Recommendations

Immediately after the inauguration of President Trump on January 20, 2025, he will face a series of critical and immediate challenges: immigrants, the economy, energy prices, national security, the Russia/Ukraine and Israel/Gaza wars, China/Taiwan, the de-Dollarization efforts of the BRICS-Nations, and the list does not end here.

The Trump Administration must immediately have an effective, coherent, and comprehensive economic plan based on Zero Cost Economics, and everyone must know about it. Think of housing, "Prosperity-Inducing Incomes," a strategy to reduce inflation, and all the other points described here earlier.

Simply defeating Kamala Harris will not make the Trump Administration great unless it is ready to immediately implement such plans that will benefit everyone. Together, we can formulate the plans and strategies for a landslide election and fulfill these promises as well.

Most, if not all, of the illegal immigrants must be removed from the United States starting immediately. This is necessary for economic reasons as well as to protect unemployed Americans from low-labor-cost immigrants. We should not help illegal immigrants at the expense of the good American people. Already, Democrats have ignorantly drowned the U.S.

economy with all kinds of social costs, and the only way out would be to deport them all. And reduce the financial burden on the U.S. economy.

There are two viable options to accomplish this goal: offer them voluntary return to their own country with some financial help or make financial or other arrangements with some African or Latin American nations to send them all there.

As one of the most qualified experts on the Middle East issues, I emphasize that the road to world peace and prosperity starts in post-mullah Iran, which requires immediate attention to bring about. This is the most urgent step the Trump Administration must take to achieve lasting peace and prosperity in the Middle East and the world.

Fortunately, this can be accomplished with minimal expense and no involvement of U.S. military forces, as the conditions are right for the Iranian people themselves to overthrow the mullahs.

President Trump is the ideal person to realize that goal, with little effort on his part.

The best person to oversee this project for President Trump would be Senator Marco Rubio, as Secretary of State. As he is trusted by anti-mullah Iranians, his appointment would encourage and energize all anti-mullah regime patriots in Iran and abroad to topple the regime rapidly.

With the mullahs gone, Iranian support for Hezbollah, Hamas, the Houthis, and other terrorists would end overnight. Economically, politically, and militarily, there will be endless deals to be made with the new American-friendly regime. Among these will be the subversion of the de-dollarization plans of the BRICS nations and China's Belt and Road Initiative. Russia can be brought to leave post-mullah Iran for a good while losing a vital source of offensive weapons.

The overall goal of it is to establish a strong and vital Iran committed to peace and exporting prosperity rather than terror. This would directly benefit the U.S. and Israel, as well as Saudi Arabia and all other countries in the Middle East.

A popular referendum can be held in post-mullah Iran for the people of Iran to decide their future. Crown Prince Reza Pahlavi, son of the late Shah, supports this plan, and over 85% of the Iranian people desire a return era of the late Shah of Iran.

When the dust settles in the Middle East, the Abraham Accord, a brilliant achievement of the former Trump Administration, should be revived with a definite plan for a two-state solution for Israel and the Palestinians. However, the form under discussion and approved by the United Nations simply will not work.

Unfortunately, the Arab and Muslim representatives' responses regarding this solution were emotional and shortsighted. All the non-Arab and non-Muslim countries do not understand how things can be made to work in the Middle

East due to their lack of understanding of Middle East regional dynamics.

Creating a Palestinian state directly bordering Israel will never work and will be fatal for the world. If this solution is ever attempted, it would guarantee the nuclear annihilation of the world. At least, world peace and prosperity will never happen.

The real and prudent solution lies in the creation of two super states: the United States of Israel, with all the Arab countries in the region, and the United States of Iran (post-mullah-regime Iran), with all the countries in the East and Northeast of Iran. There is a detailed prudent plan for this solution to create peace and prosperity in the Middle East and North Africa. To realize this or any other plans, the new Trump Administration needs unquestionably the cooperation of Israel's Prime Minister Benjamin "Bibi" Netanyahu, as a staunch partner, not only to resolve the Middle East but also for all other issues, particularly the challenges posed by the BRICS Nations.

American production of crude oil and natural gas must be stimulated in the United States to bring energy prices down to revive the economy and fulfill all of President Trump's economic plans. American production must provide total self-sufficiency to never again be threatened by OPEC, Russia, or anyone else.

Oil policy can be used to achieve many critical American economic and political goals, including dealing with Russia, China, India, and others. Oil policy is the key to foiling the de-dollarization efforts of the BRICS nations and discouraging other nations from applying to join the BRICS bloc.

The U.S. Dollar must retain its dominant position as the main reserve currency. De-dollarization efforts are aimed at dethroning the dollar. However, no currency or basket of currencies can replace the dollar — so far — unless we allow it to happen by lack of diligence or by stupid monetary policy; no nation in the world can still take over America's place individually or collectively.

In fact, the currency and economic experts of the BRICS nations seem not to understand what their real goal should be other than simply to replace the dollar with their own weaker, less desirable currencies. Note: I would remind readers in 1975, I was the person who suggested to the Shah of Iran that requiring partial payment in Iranian Rials would improve Iran's position in terms of trade in oil exports.

As the Trump Administration takes control over critical issues, it is highly recommended to create a new U.S. Department of the Economy, which would also encompass the Department of the Treasury and its agencies, including the Internal Revenue Service, as well as the Securities and Exchange Commission.

We should abolish the Federal Reserve and replace it with an institution that is not owned by banks who, initially more than anyone, benefit from the Fed's obsolete and shortsighted policies — at the expense of all the rest of us, which eventually leads to their collapse. This is easier said than done, but it is necessary to enact monetary policy — and other policies and controls beyond simply setting interest rates — to achieve permanent economic prosperity and security for all Americans without inflation and consequential debt.

North Atlantic Treaty Organization (NATO), a military alliance of 30 countries in Europe and North America, must be converted to an economic alliance between existing member countries by having Russia and Ukraine join them in the interest of peace in that region. Simultaneously, efforts must be made to reduce the expansion of the destructive military power of this organization by redirecting it to developing and expanding the capabilities and readiness of the member nations to be made present in combating natural disasters, wherever they may occur in the member countries and possibly in non-member nations. Doing so can help affected nations and their people recover from natural disasters. At the same time, it'll become an attractive source of revenue for involved businesses by doing useful, constructive, and peaceful work instead of creating rising social costs of all kinds for wasting all the resources for the readiness of potentially destructive, fatal war, which no one gain from it no matter how one looks at it.

Similarly, the United Nations must eventually be resolved and replaced by nations that fulfill at least these two conditions:

1) Political and religious Parties are replaced by "Specialized Parties" in the areas that the nation needs.

   (Note: This will eliminate thugs, looters, murderers, killers, dictators (religious, civil, or military), incompetent and unqualified people who ever get to a leading position. Only "Zerocrats," experts with detailed spelled-out plans based on Zero Cost Economics, can be elected.)

2) Candidates are elected by the members of the respective specialized parties.

   (Note: Not based votes on votes from non-members of the respective part.)

This step can be taken after the changes made in NATO and the necessary arrangements and agreements are made with a series of other countries in Asia, Africa, and Latin America.

Conventional politics and political systems, just as conventional economics and economic systems, have failed miserably!

These fundamental changes provide a foundation to build upon. They will enable the implementation of many prosperity-inducing policies and avoid the structural tendency built into our economy to transfer wealth and income to a tiny minority at the expense of everyone else; all we must do is implement a series of sound and effective economic-monetary policies to change the existing rising recurring social costs of all kinds to rising social benefits of all kinds for people at practically ZERO COST—it doesn't cost, it pays!

My forthcoming books will detail more of these common-sense policies.

Conclusion

If the Trump campaign is equipped with the right economic plans, not only will President Trump win the election in a landslide, but he will be positioned to overcome the challenges caused by the incompetence of the Biden administration.

If Republican Congressional candidates campaign on the same page as President Trump, the resulting strong Republican majorities in the U.S. House and Senate will facilitate and streamline the implementation of the policies described here and much more.

Along the way, we can undo the wrongs of the Carter, Obama, and Biden administrations in the Middle East and the United States. Carter replaced the late Shah of Iran, the best friend America ever had in the Middle East, with the barbaric Ayatollah Ruhollah Khomeini. The result was a cascade of chaos, violence, war, and terrorism in the Middle East that continues to this day.

Millions of innocent people in the Middle East and thousands of Americans died, with countless more disabled and maimed for the rest of their lives. It is no secret that Obama and Biden brought Muslims to every corner of America.

Ending the wrongdoings of these three presidents will begin a new era of peace and prosperity in the Middle East and the United States — and will lead the world in that direction.

The United States can resume its role of world leadership, which has suffered since the Obama Administration to this date, except during the brief four years of the Trump Administration.

I sincerely wish President Trump all the health, strength, and support he will need to complete his highly essential mission. He may not be a perfect man, but he is the man of the hour America needs.

He is the man and the hope for the United States, all Americans, and all the people of the world.

Biography

Farid A. Khavari

PhD. Economist

"Raising interest rates to fight inflation is like using gasoline to fight fire."

EDUCATION

- **Doctorate in Economics and Political Sciences**
  University of Bremen, Germany, 1976.
  Dissertation: *The Pricing of OPEC Crude Oil – An Analysis of the Determinants*,
  the world's first doctoral dissertation about OPEC.

- **Master's Degree in Economics and Social Sciences**
  University of Hamburg, Germany, 1973.
  Thesis: *The Interdependence of the Oil-Producing and Oil-Consuming Nations*,
  the world's first master's thesis about OPEC.

LANGUAGES

English, German, Persian, Dari, Hindi

PLACES OF BIRTH AND RESIDENCE

Born: Yazd, Iran 1943
Iran: 1943 – 1945
India: 1946 – 1954
Iran: 1954 – 1964
Germany: 1964 – 1977
Miami, Florida, United States: 1977 – to present.

PROFESSION

Independent economist for over 47 years, author of 10 books.
1977 – 2020 owned various successful small businesses in the manufacturing and service sectors.
Patents:

- Solar Heating check valve and flow indicator, U.S. Patent # 4474209
- Design for an orthopedic pillow, U.S. Patent # D306245

"Marxism, Keynesianism, Monetarism, and all other conventional economics have failed miserably because they are inflationary and debt-inducing.

Now is the time for non-inflationary, and non-debt-inducing Zero Cost Economics."

Farid A. Khavari
Unconventional Economist
Creator of Zero Cost Economics

CANDIDATE FOR PUBLIC OFFICES

- Candidate for Florida Governor in 2010 and 2014 ballots
- Candidate for Miami-Dade County Mayor in 2012 and 2016 ballots

I was the first Iranian American candidate ever who:

- Ran for the highest political office in the third largest U.S. state.
- Was the only candidate to present my detailed platform in a 160-page book, made available to the public for free download.
- Refused several offers from big money groups, relying only on personal funds and small individual contributions for my campaigns. I maintained my independence to work in the interest of the people.
- Across the United States, many candidates from both parties adopted parts of my economic plans for their platforms, especially my proposal for publicly owned state banks.

21st-Century American Economists

LISTED AMONG THE TOP 21ST-Century American Economists by FAMOUS FIX (ranked # 7)

UNIQUE STRENGTH

As a keen observer of great people in my challenging life, I learned that to accomplish great things, one cannot be corrupt. This is especially true in politics, where one person's corruption can impact the lives of millions of people. The strongest powers that can lead anyone to accomplish great things are honesty and integrity. Of course, one must be competent and qualified for the job at hand, too.

- During my 2010 campaign for Florida governor, I was contacted by a representative of Hojat-ul-Islam Ali-Akbar Rafsanjani, the former president of the Islamic Republic of Iran and one of the three leaders of the 1979 revolution with Ayatollahs Khomeini and Khamanei. He offered me $200 million, a private jet, a mansion, a week's shopping spree in Paris, and the promise to be elected governor. I refused vigorously. Money was never the driving force in my life, and doing dirty work is no way to good work for the people.
- In my 2012 campaign for Miami-Dade County mayor, a Chinese entrepreneur offered me $2 million to support my campaign, in exchange for county contracts after my election. I refused this also. I was running to serve people and to create a model that could be emulated worldwide, not just to win the office.
- After all of my campaigns for governor and mayor, I refunded leftover donations to the donors, which got me overwhelming compliments and praise. Honesty and integrity are the two strong columns on which one can always lean.

MEETINGS WITH WORLD LEADERS

Mahatma Gandhi, India's spiritual and political leader. My father took me to see him in 1947. Although I was a small child, I never forgot this experience.

Jawaharlal Nehru, Indian prime minister. I met him at the Iranian Embassy in New Delhi together with Tensing Norgay, the conqueror of Mount Everest (1953).

In 1976 I had a personal audience with the **Shah of Iran**, discussing coupling of oil revenues paid partially in Iranian rials to improve Iran's terms-of-trade

instead of raising oil prices, which would lead to rising inflation and worsening of terms-of-trade. Now the BRICS nations are pursuing this concept to de-dollarize their trade.

Also in 1976, I met with Iranian **Prime Minister Amir-Abbas Howeida**, the greatest and most honest Prime Minister of the Shah's era.

In 2014, I met Iranian **Crown Prince Reza Pahlavi**.

WITNESSING HISTORY

- On January 30, 1948, Mahatma Gandhi was assassinated. My grandmother and I were among the crowd saying farewell as his body was carried to India's Parliament.
- As a child I witnessed the decolonization of India from England. I was deeply impressed by the people's determination to refuse serving British rulers in India or buying British made products.
- Most disturbing during my time in India were the times on my way to and from school when I witnessed the sudden outbreak of mob violence between Muslims and Hindus and the following massacre of each other.
- In the early 1960s I was witness to the Shah's White Revolution in Iran. I served in the Education Corps from 1962 – 1964.
- In 1968, inspired by Robert Kennedy's campaign for president, I came to Los Angeles, CA to study, to pursue my dream in bodybuilding and support him. I was outside the Ambassador Hotel when Kennedy was shot, and a dream became a nightmare. A few months later, I returned to Germany to finish my studies there.

EARLY ACHIEVEMENTS

During the rule of the late Shah of Iran, I was one of the first to join the new Education Corps. I taught children and adults reading, writing, and arithmetic in a small village in northern Iran from 1962 to 1964. At age 19, as a high school graduate in the Corps, I accomplished the following:

- Built a four-classroom school just by mobilizing villagers to help, with no financial assistance from the government or any other source.
- Taught 60 children and adults reading, writing and arithmetic.
- Taught the villagers to grow new crops including cantaloupe and watermelon.
- Built a public bath area for villagers' use by mobilizing villagers.
- Created a volleyball court for the children by engaging them to build a volleyball net.
- Outlawed the extortionate 100% annual interest rates imposed on the villagers by a rich man. This discouraged people from working just to pay all their earnings to this man. I freed the villagers from this crippling interest with mediation and reasoning. The next day I was attacked by a hired thug but escaped serious injury.

In 1964, I left Iran with only a bus ticket from Tehran to Munich, Germany, two blankets, a $100 bill, and a gold ring which my father gave me. I went to Germany and worked my way through university to a Ph.D. in Economics. In the process I accomplished a series of other things (see below). Today, I still have those two blankets and the ring my father gave me.

DEALING WITH REAL-LIFE ISSUES

The foundation of my training in economics was set in many areas:

- The most profound impact of my life that shaped my future views was a real-life experience that took me from affluence to extreme poverty, as we were forced to return to Iran with nothing when India was decolonized and rising back to the level that I have achieved everything I ever wanted in my life.
- I studied the full range of views in economics—I earned my master's degree in economics at a very conservative university (University of Hamburg, Germany) and Ph.D. from a very liberal/Marxist university (University of Bremen, Germany). This prepared me to understand both the fundamental principles, and the shortcomings, of the various economic philosophies of the world.

I worked at the three most prominent economic institutes in Germany:

a) I worked in the Monetary and Currency Department of the Hamburg Economic Institute under Prof. Hans-Eckart Scharrer. I followed the development of the interest rates and currencies of the major countries and converted the data into daily graphs and charts. The unique knowledge and expertise I acquired during this period enabled me to understand economics from a different perspective and provided me with a vision to develop my later concepts in economics. These developments included the concepts of coupling of oil-producing countries' currencies as partial payments for oil exports; the concepts of Zero Cost Economics; defining productivity in the service sectors; productivity-, and prosperity-inducing models for Super-Banks and Super-Clinics, etc.

b) The Institute had a vast library of economic books and archives covering every conceivable topic dealing with economics, trade, business, environment, energy, and many other related issues. I took advantage of my access to this rich source of information to expand my knowledge and understanding of these important topics.

c) After graduation, I worked at the Institute for Technological Development in Hamburg. My job was to read all the publications and collect information about the newest developments in technology, economics, energy, raw materials, environment, etc. and to write summaries for the multi-national German conglomerates who sponsored the Institute. This was an incredible opportunity to be paid to learn about the latest developments in many important fields.

d) During this period, I had another great opportunity to learn from a master: Prof. Alfons Lemper, the Head of the German Overseas Institute. I published two books at that institute for which Prof. Lemper wrote the forewords.

e) During this period, I was the Economics and Energy editor of the *VDI Nachrichten*, the largest weekly publication for German Engineers.

My business experience started in 1977 when I came to the United States. I learned to develop and sell products and services and ran a few successful small businesses. My focus in business was not only on making money, but to improve everything I could. This interest led not only to patents on various products and development of many other products such as evacuated high temperature solar tubes, heat exchangers, exercise equipment, etc., but also to development of the concepts of Zero Cost Economics, Zero Cost Enterprises, Zero Cost Cities, the definition of productivity in the service sector, Economic Security Indices, etc.

My background combined with my life experiences led to new economic concepts, and to a new understanding of old concepts. I can apply these concepts to devise an economic plan tailored to achieve any specific desired results, such as creation of jobs without cost to taxpayers, as well as the greater overall goal of sustainably growing prosperity and economic security for all the people in the economy. Conversely, this knowledge enables analysis of any economic plan to predict its outcome.

ALWAYS AHEAD OF MY TIME

From 1960 to 1964, at age 17, I wrote a full-page weekly column about bodybuilding and nutrition for a national sports magazine, *Kayhane Verzeshi*. During this period, I was juicing vegetables and fruits and drinking it for health and bodybuilding reasons years before Jack LaLanne started with his juicer in America and made it popular.

In 1964 at the age of 19, during my time in the Education Corps, I wrote a book about experiences and suggestions, and presented it to Iran's Education Ministry under the Shah, for which I received third prize.

I wrote an unpublished book in 1973 for the late Shah of Iran dealing with terms-of-trade issues. I advised coupling oil exports to payment in Iranian rials, regardless of oil prices based on U.S. dollars. This would have resulted in rising revenues in real terms for Iran.

Later, in my 1976 dissertation, I proposed the coupling of the oil exporting nations' currencies to their oil exports to improve their terms of trade. 48 years passed before a variation of that proposal was implemented in different, but improper and ineffective way for the first time by Russia and China in dealing with the Islamic Republic of Iran for oil transactions. Recently, we hear more about it as the Russia-Ukraine war escalates and sanctions of all kinds are implemented. Plans for "de-dollarization" make daily headlines with no understanding of how it should be done to be effective and long-lasting. It's no secret that Saddam Hussein and Moammar Ghaddafi both tried to challenge the U.S. dollar and failed due to U.S. invasions of Iraq and Libya. However, BRICS Nations will also not succeed because they do not understand the interrelation of all the economic factors involved; they all, like the rest of the world, believe an economy is an aggregation of businesses, which it is not. Businesses are just one of many economic factors involved in an economy. The other factors are energy, environment, technology, raw materials, agriculture, politics, legislation, social and religious issues, trade, natural disasters, standard of living, and most importantly all the recurring costs and social costs of all kinds associated with these factors. A nation can have many successful, world-class businesses but a failed economy. The goals of an economy differ from those of businesses and vice versa. They run counter to each other. This perilous ignorance is the root of many problems confronting the economies of all nations in the world.

In 1975 the Deutsches Uebersee-Institut, a German research institute involved in researching the world economic problems, published my book, *Die Oelpreispolitic der OPEC-Laender – Grenzen, Gruende und Hintergruende (The Oil Price Policy of the OPEC Countries — Limits, Reasons and Background).*

In 1976 the Institute also published my next book, *Die OPEC im weltwirtschaftlichen Spannungsfeld – Ein Beitrag zur Diskussion um die "neue Weltwirtschaftsordnung." (OPEC in global economic tensions - A contribution to the discussion about the "new world economic order.")*

In my doctoral dissertation, published by the University of Bremen in 1977, I wrote that no substitution for oil will ever occur simply due to the rising crude oil prices. The common perception was that rising oil prices would lead to substitution of crude oil by alternative energy sources and technology, and reduced demand for oil. However, oil prices rose from $10 per barrel to over $150, yet no serious substitution for crude oil has been implemented. In fact, demand for oil continues to rise to this day.

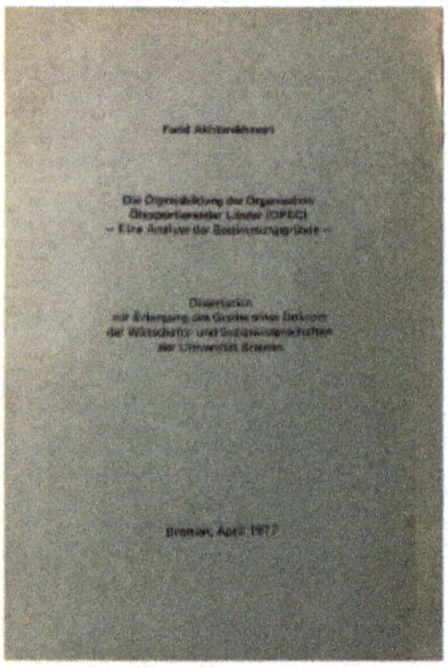

My 1990 book, ***Vultures: Doctors, Lawyers, Hospitals, and Insurance Companies***, warned of skyrocketing health care costs in the U.S. and proposed Super-Clinics and other solutions for affordable quality healthcare for everyone at much lower costs.

My other 1990 book, ***Oil & Islam: The Ticking Bomb*** emphasized that the real threat to the West is the Islamic Republic of Iran, with Iraq being "the lesser evil." After 45 years, countless lives, and trillions of dollars wasted in Iraq, Iran is still the main threat.

On November 17, 1993, the *Miami Herald* published my article about NAFTA alongside those of prominent leaders such as AFL-CIO President Lane Kirkland, President Cesar Gaviria-Trujillo of Colombia, and others. Excerpt: "...As the economy moves toward full employment, projects like NAFTA can be implemented successfully for all nations involved. NAFTA, in its current form, could well result in innocent and dedicated workers moving from the upper middle class to the welfare rolls. What is accomplished if Wal-Mart or Chrysler hits the jackpot only at the expense of the working people of both nations?"

Environomics: The Economics of Environmentally Safe Prosperity (1993) explained that we can have sustainable economic growth without harming the environment, and how to do it — the first book on the economics of the environment.

In 1995 my first work of fiction, ***The Final Reckoning**: **The Islamic Plot to Destroy the Dollar***, showed how the U.S. dollar could be destroyed by the Islamic countries, primarily the Islamic Republic of Iran.

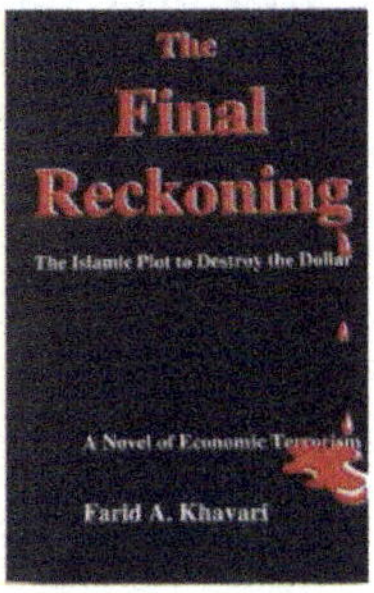

On August 1, 1995, my *Miami Herald* article **"Iran's threat to the Mideast is a threat to the world"** warned of the threat from the Islamic Republic of Iran.

With the threat from the Islamic Republic of Iran and a looming recession in 2009, I published ***Towards a Zero Cost Economy*** to show the way to independence from oil and to create general prosperity and economic security. This book presented my platform for the Florida governor's race. Zero Cost Economics focuses on creating environmentally safe and sustainable economic growth without inflation by reducing and eliminating recurring costs of all kinds. Zero Cost Economics leads to rising general prosperity and economic security for all people and businesses. This, in turn, reduces social costs. Zero Cost Economics avoids inflation, growing debt, extreme inequality, and rising poverty which are inevitable results of all conventional economic models, whether capitalist or socialist.

My 2011 book ***The Final Crash*** predicted the end of U.S. dominance in the Middle East in 2013. As we have witnessed, since that time, the U.S. has been increasingly retreating in the world. In this book I also showed the roadmap to a strong America.

In 2015, the Iran Nuclear Deal was seen as a choice between nuclear containment or war. I proposed a third option: peaceful regime change by the Iranian people themselves. In a paper directed to U.S. policymakers, I detailed the conditions that make Iran ripe for regime change and how it can occur without foreign involvement. War with Iran is out of the question. A U.S.-friendly regime in Iran would neutralize any nuclear threat, defuse tensions in the Middle East, cancel support for terrorism, recognize and trade with Israel, and strengthen the U.S. dollar's faltering position as the preeminent reserve currency in the world. However, in reality the Iran Nuclear Deal was a hoax used to launder $150 billion.

BOOKS PUBLISHED

- **The Final Crash: The End of U.S. Dominance in 2013,** Morris Publishing, Kearney, NE. U.S.A., 2011
- **Towards a Zero Cost Economy – A Blueprint to Create General Economic Security in a Carefree Economy**, iUniverse, Bloomington, IN, U.S.A., 2009
- **The Final Reckoning – The Islamic Plot to Destroy the Dollar** (fiction), Morris Publishing, Kearney, NE, U.S.A., 1995
- **Environomics – The Economics of Environmentally Safe Prosperity,** Praeger, Westport, CT, U.S.A., 1993
- **Oil & Islam – The Ticking Bomb,** Roundtable, CA, U.S.A., 1990
- **Vultures – Doctors, Lawyers, Hospitals and Insurance Companies,** Roundtable, CA, U.S.A., 1990

- **Die OPEC im weltwirtschaftlichen Spannungsfeld – Ein Beitrag zur Discussion um die "neue Weltwirtschaftsordnung"** (OPEC and the New World Economic Order), Institut fuer Allgemeine Ueberseeforschung, Hamburg, Germany, 1976

- **Die Oelpreispolitik der OPEC-Laender – Grenzen, Gruende und Hintergruende** (The Oil Price Policy of the OPEC Countries – Limits, Reasons and Backgrounds), Institut fuer Allgemeine Ueberseeforschung, Hamburg, Germany, 1975.

- **Die Oelkrisen bedrohen den Wohlstand des Westens** (The Oil Crises Threaten the Prosperity of the West), (manuscript) Germany, 1973. This book was given to the Shah of Iran in 1975 as recommendations for moderation in OPEC pricing policy.

- **Sepahe danesh dar rahe sazendegiye roustaha** (Education Corps in Building Villages), Iran, 1964.

SELECTED PAPERS

- *A Great Economy for Iran: Prosperity, and Economic Security for All Iranians, Economic Justice and A Fair Share for Everyone*, March 1, 2018

- *A Third Option for Iran: Regime Change without War, an opportunity for peaceful regime change by the Iranian people themselves* (2015)

SELECTED PAPERS, continued

- *The Zero Cost Cities Project: A Blueprint to Create Massive Wealth and Employment* (2014)
- *The Road to a Prosperous and Modern Iran – Democracy and Economic Security as Constitutional Rights of All Iranians* (2013)
- *Productivity-Inducing Competition (PIC) – The Key to Universal and Affordable Healthcare* (1993)
- *Interest Rates: The Silver Bullet, a Practical Solution to Revitalize the U.S. Economy and Reduce the Federal Deficit* (1992)
- *The Key to Economic Recovery and Lasting Prosperity* (1992)

JOURNAL, NEWSPAPER & BLOG ARTICLES

Numerous articles about economics, environment, healthcare, energy, oil, raw materials, financing, banking, outsourcing, insourcing, corruption, social benefits and social profits, costs, and social costs appeared in the following publications:

- Brennstoffspiegel (Germany)
- Development and Corporation (Germany)
- Die Welt (Germany)
- Ekonomska Analiza (former Yugoslavia)

- Frankfurter Rundschau (Germany)
- Internationale Entwicklung (Germany)
- Handelsblatt (Germany)
- Maandschrift Economie (The Netherlands)
- Tehran Economist (Iran)
- The Miami Herald (United States)
- VDI Nachrichten (Germany)
- OEN – OpEd News (USA)
- InvestmentWatch.com (USA)
- Gold Coast Chronicle (USA)

MEDIA APPEARANCES

TELEVISION

20/20 with Barbara Walters (ABC, USA)

Geraldo Rivera Show (NBC, USA)

Rick Sanchez (Fox News, Miami, FL)

Numerous Iranian TV channels in Los Angeles, CA

RADIO

Numerous interviews on radio shows throughout the United States to discuss my books and economic solutions, welcomed by conservative as well as liberal broadcasters.

Periodic guest on Frank Mottek radio show, a famous business anchor for CBS Los Angeles (KNX1070 News radio) in Los Angeles, CA for my opinion on economic developments.

Made in the USA
Monee, IL
03 November 2026

67381181R00079